TEAM BARRIERS

Actions for Overcoming the Blocks to Empowerment, Involvement, & High-Performance

D1476668

BY

ANN & BOB HARPER

From the authors of SUCCEEDING AS A SELF-DIRECTED WORK TEAM: 20 Important Questions Answered and SKILL-BUILDING FOR SELF-DIRECTED TEAM MEMBERS: A Complete Course—a new book/workbook examining why most change efforts fail and how to make sure yours succeeds!

MW Corporation

Team Barriers:
Actions for Overcoming the Blocks to
Empowerment, Involvement,
& High-Performance

by Ann & Bob Harper

Printed and bound in the United States of America
Library of Congress Card #94-75110
ISBN: 1-880859-03-3

To order additional copies, call MW Corporation at 914-528-0888.
Quantity discounts available. (See Section Eleven of this book for
information on this and other books, videos, and training.)

SPECIAL THANKS
To MW Corporation Associate:

Sharon Bretti

> "Two-thirds of all quality programs studied stalled or failed to produce the desired results."
> —McKinsey & Co. study, as reported in Training Magazine (Nov. 1993)

> ". . . 50% to 70% of the organizations that undertake a reengineering effort do not achieve the dramatic results they intended."
> —Michael Hammer & James Champy, authors of *Reengineering the Corporation.*

Why Do Most Change Efforts Fail
And How Do You Make Sure Yours Succeeds?

In *TEAM BARRIERS: Actions for Overcoming the Blocks to EMPOWERMENT, INVOLVEMENT, & HIGH-PERFORMANCE,* Ann & Bob Harper dare to discuss the very real challenges organizations face when implementing change efforts. In this, their third book, they examine the planning, implementing, maintaining, and renewal that High-Performing Teams must have if they are to succeed.

Whether you're attempting TQM, PIT, CQI, Self-Directed/Self-Managing/High-Performing Teams; whether you've redesigned or reengineered—overcoming these barriers is the key.

Turning traditional hierarchical organizations into High-Performance models is critical to success, even survival, in today's competitive environment.

This book/workbook is an ACTION PLAN for succeeding at EMPOWERMENT, INVOLVEMENT, & HIGH-PERFORMANCE.

About the Authors:

Ann Harper, associate at MW Corporation, has taught, consulted with, and written about organizational transformation for the past ten years. Helping organizations transition to high-performance models has been very exciting and personally satisfying for Ann. She has custom-designed training in the areas of: High-performing/self-directed teams, leadership, facilitation, team building, motivation, active listening, change/transition, and quality customer service. Ann and Bob are married to each other and often work together. They have co-authored other books/workbooks: *Succeeding As a Self-Directed Work Team: 20 Important Questions Answered; Skill-Building for S-D Team Members: A Complete Course;* "Self-Directed Teams & Your Organization: Two Assessment Tools." Ann and Bob live in Yorktown, a suburb of New York City.

Bob Harper, President of MW Corporation, has worked with organizations for more than twenty years. After working for GE, GM, and IC Industries, he formed MW Corporation, a full service consulting firm. Bob has been teaching about employee involvement, empowerment, and high-performance for years. More recently, he feels American organizations are finally listening to him, and more importantly, to their employees. Bob has worked with thousands of people (individuals and teams) in various organizations all over the country. His books are the result of this first-hand, practical experience. Above all,

Bob is a teacher, trainer, educator who helps people find meaning through their work.

ABOUT MW CORPORATION: Your Partners In Learning

MW Corporation is a full-service consulting firm founded in 1983. It provides training (public workshops and custom-designed on-site workshops), books, workbooks, assessments, and videos. Specializing in teams, empowerment, participative leadership, and high-performance, MW Corporation designs and delivers workshops on: High-performing/self-directed teams, team leadership, management, supervision, facilitation, active listening, and quality customer service. The guiding belief of the company is that human beings have unlimited potential and our training, books, videos help develop the "human resource." People are the greatest asset any organization has and investing in people is the only way to create competitive advantage. A partial list of clients includes: AT&T, GE, Compaq, General Motors, Northern Telecom, Johnson & Johnson, EDS, Microsoft, Exxon, Steelcase, BellSouth, IRS, Texas Instruments, Coors Brewing, Digital, Hewlett-Packard, Intel, Harris Semiconductor, Bell Canada, American Express, WalMart, Target Stores, 3M, Dupont, Corning, Alcoa, TRW, Xerox.

MW Corporation *"Your Partners In Learning"*

3150 Lexington Ave., Mohegan Lake, NY 10547
914-528-0888   Fax: 914-528-8889

This book/workbook was written for and designed to be used by:

- Team Members
- Team Leaders
- Managers/Supervisors
- Trainers
- Facilitators
- Consultants
- Top Management
- Educators
- OD, HR People
- Organizations:
  —that are planning a change effort and want to learn how to do it "right"
  —that have reengineered their processes and want to maximize the results from their teams
  —that have started change efforts and are experiencing problems
  —whose teams have plateaued
  —that failed with past change efforts and this time want to overcome the blocks
  —that have to succeed (their survival depends on it)

Purpose of This Book:

- To help individuals & organizations understand what **EMPOWERMENT, INVOLVEMENT, & HIGH-PERFORMANCE** really are
- To explain why achieving these qualities is critical to the survival of all American organizations (whether they're in manufacturing, service, the government, not-for-profit, or education)
- To describe the barriers you'll encounter (sooner or later) and provide ACTIONS that can mean the difference between moving ahead, stopping, or going back
- To provide training materials for everyone in the work force: teams, individuals, & leaders
- To provide exercises, assessments, and checklists for involving everyone in the learning required for successful change efforts (whether you're calling it TQM, CI, Reengineering, Redesign, Process Improvement, Problem-solving, or Self-Directed Teams)
- To provide activities for:
  - building **PARTNERSHIPS** with unions, workers, customers, vendors, & suppliers
  - developing **HIGH-PERFORMANCE TEAMS**
  - assessing how **EMPOWERED** you/ your teams really are
- To help develop strategies for successfully dealing with barriers (turning challenges into opportunities)

- To help people redesign/reengineer/ recreate their organizations
- To help reengineering efforts succeed in producing the breakthroughs they're capable of providing
- To help Facilitators maximize the potential of their teams
- To help Team Leaders learn what teams need to make them "high-performing"
- To help Team Members learn how to overcome the barriers preventing their teams from achieving maximum effectiveness
- To provide information and models of **EMPOWERMENT, INVOLVEMENT, & HIGH-PERFORMANCE**

In the last ten years, most organizations have embarked on some type of employee involvement change effort. These have gone by many names:

- TQM
- CQI
- Suggestion Systems
- Employee Surveys
- Problem-Solving Teams
- Process Improvement Teams
- High-Involvement/Self-Directed/Self-Managed Teams
- Project Teams/Task Forces for Reengineering

All of these efforts, although they have different names, aim for similar results:

- Streamlining work processes
- Tapping the ideas, skills, and expertise of all workers
- Fixing problems & satisfying customers
- Involving everyone in sharing responsibility, commitment, & participation
- Pushing decisions down to the people who should be making them
- Lowering costs, reducing time, and improving quality by redesigning/ reengineering work processes
- Creating "good jobs" for everyone (work that has wholeness, meaning, variety, challenge, & growth)
- Increasing motivation, morale, & work satisfaction
- Adding more leadership to everyone's job

The aim of this book/workbook is to examine what often goes wrong with these efforts:

Why do *most* change efforts fail?

Why has it been so difficult to achieve empowerment, involvement, and high-performance despite the fact that everyone agrees they're needed and organizations have spent a lot of time and money on all sorts of "programs?"

The actions we present for overcoming these barriers are based on our experience in over twenty years of consulting with various types of organizations. Each section will describe a major barrier and focus on the actions needed to overcome it, so it won't slow you down or stop your progress.

C O N T E N T S

"American business and American workers must
make a commitment to go beyond the slogans
and get down to the hard but essential work
of building high-performance organizations
where both responsibility and rewards
are widely shared."

Robert Reich
Secretary of Labor
(Quoted from a letter to the editor,
Inc. Magazine, August 1993)

INTRODUCTION

We began writing about what we saw happening in American industry back in 1989. Our experience, then as now, was based on working with thousands of people from various types of organizations. We feel that since '89 many things have happened and some of them have been very heartening:

- Teams, like motherhood and apple pie, are now viewed as "good" to have
- Most companies will tell you they have teams of one sort or another
- CEOs say they want empowerment, involvement, and high-performance
- Consultants agree on empowered teams as the basic organizational building block of any successful company
- Organizations of all types are attempting to "reinvent" themselves
- Workers agree that empowerment is just common sense because it acknowledges their capabilities as "thinkers" not just "doers"
- Unions are giving teams a try (and some are even leading the way)
- Pay-for-performance experiments are taking place

- Evidence keeps mounting that employee involvement, quality, empowerment, and teams are critical to the success of any organization
- Service industries are trying concepts that worked in manufacturing
- Schools, the military, government, churches, are all experimenting with shared decision-making, empowering frontline teams, eliminating wasteful, non-value added efforts, etc.
- Everywhere, departments and functions are giving way to reengineered core processes that save time, money, etc.
- Everything about work is being rethought and redesigned

But, we also see many signs that are distressing:

- A lot of "talk" about making America more competitive and the need for training everyone in the work force, but not enough time and money spent on making this a reality
- CEOs advocating empowerment, but not understanding what massive change is involved
- Top management delegating the

leadership of change to others and then wondering why failure resulted from lack of commitment

- Managers being ordered to form teams and doing it with little understanding or enthusiasm
- Supervisors being removed before they've had a chance to develop self-directed teams
- Little or no change in the attitudes, philosophies, assumptions and values driving organizations
- Not enough training before teams start and not enough afterwards
- Not enough involvement in the planning and implementation of change efforts by *all* the key stakeholders: customers, union, workers, managers, supervisors, and support people

As we see it, the key question facing us at the close of the twentieth century is:

Are American organizations fundamentally changing or are TQM, empowerment, involvement, self-direction just more "programs" that failed?

It's too soon to answer this question. We want this book to be an honest look at the barriers we have experienced in the last ten years working with organizations. The actions we present can work—we've seen them work—in organizations willing to try them.

We think overcoming the barriers to empowerment, involvement, and high-performance is essential to any organization's survival. **America is at a crossroads where critical choices need to be made:**

Choice #1: We can stay as we are and not change. This is the easiest road and the one most organizations have taken. But as history has proven, this choice means eventually losing to competitors who have not stood still.

Choice #2: We can take the cost-cutting, downsizing road that we read about in the paper every day. We can try to compete with the cheapest labor in the world and pay our people as little as possible. This is not a formula for producing quality. This road leads to continued decline in the American standard of living as we watch "good" jobs disappear.

Choice #3: The third choice is the hardest because it means overcoming barriers and changing almost everything (our assumptions, attitudes, structures, and practices), but it's the only choice that will give us long-range competitive advantage. We can listen to our customers, listen to our employees, redesign/reengineer our traditional, bureaucratic organizations, and then train our people to work "smarter" so we can compete with any country in the world.

There's a lot of bad news every day about layoffs, downsizing, etc., but despite this, the good news is that for some companies crisis has caused rethinking and redesign. Americans have always had a knack for creativity, innovation, and risk-taking. All these qualities are needed today in overcoming the barriers that are preventing us from achieving what we must have in order to be successful: real empowerment, employee involvement, and high-performance. Finally, the time is right for creating democratic workplaces where partnerships exist between employees, customers, vendors, and suppliers.

ACTION ONE

Empowering Everyone

- *High-Involvement Exercise:*

  How Empowered Are You?

  How Empowered Is Your Team?
  - *Assessment*
  - *Consensus-Building Activity*

- *Empowerment: A Definition*

- *Barriers to Empowerment*

- *Types of Employee Involvement & Degree of Empowerment*

- *Barriers to Development of High-Performing Teams*
  - *High-Involvement Exercise: Identifying & Overcoming Barriers*

HIGH-INVOLVEMENT EXERCISE:

How Empowered Are You?
How Empowered Is Your Team?

Learning Objective:

To assess how empowered you are as an individual and/or as a team by your organization and to agree on actions that would increase your level of empowerment.

Directions:

Step One- Individual Exercise

After reading each question, decide the **EXTENT TO WHICH THE STATEMENT IS TRUE** for you as an individual and/or your team, and circle the appropriate number.

0	1	2	3	4	5
NOT true	true to LOW extent				true to HIGH extent

1. All information needed to perform excellent work (cost-effective, high-quality, etc.) is provided.

0	1	2	3	4	5
	LOW				HIGH

2. Training has been provided on quality concepts and tools.

0	1	2	3	4	5
	LOW				HIGH

3. Information is communicated on all aspects of the total business (goals, costs, standards, customer satisfaction, etc.)

0	1	2	3	4	5
	LOW				HIGH

4. Technical training/cross-training is provided so everyone is multi-skilled and can do many jobs.

0	1	2	3	4	5
	LOW				HIGH

(*continued*)

5. Interpersonal/team training (communication, problem-solving, high-performance, team development, decision-making, conflict management, effective meetings) has been provided.

0	1	2	3	4	5
	LOW				HIGH

6. Administrative tasks that traditional supervision used to do are now done by me/my team.

0	1	2	3	4	5
	LOW				HIGH

7. There is a transition plan in place so everyone knows that empowerment will continue.

0	1	2	3	4	5
	LOW				HIGH

8. Individuals and teams develop work goals/objectives that align with overall company business goals.

0	1	2	3	4	5
	LOW				HIGH

9. Worker's ideas are listened to, recognized, and implemented.

0	1	2	3	4	5
	LOW				HIGH

10. Decisions on the daily schedule and work procedures are made by the workers themselves.

0	1	2	3	4	5
	LOW				HIGH

11. Workers measure their own work quality, quantity, service, and customer satisfaction.

0	1	2	3	4	5
	LOW				HIGH

12. Workers make decisions regarding overtime and vacation scheduling.

0	1	2	3	4	5
	LOW				HIGH

13. Team members have input on hiring and firing.

0	1	2	3	4	5
	LOW				HIGH

(*continued*)

14. Teams schedule their own team meetings.

0	1	2	3	4	5
	LOW				HIGH

15. Workers select work problems to address and recommend/implement solutions.

0	1	2	3	4	5
	LOW				HIGH

16. Peers provide feedback and appraise each other.

0	1	2	3	4	5
	LOW				HIGH

17. Workers deal directly with customers and have decision-making power to satisfy them.

0	1	2	3	4	5
	LOW				HIGH

18. Rewards are tied to performance and results (i.e., profit-sharing, pay-for-skills, gainsharing, lump-sum-bonus).

0	1	2	3	4	5
	LOW				HIGH

19. Workers feel like "owners" of this organization.

0	1	2	3	4	5
	LOW				HIGH

20. Continuous learning/training and improving is built into our culture.

0	1	2	3	4	5
	LOW				HIGH

Step Two- Team Exercise

(If you're taking this quiz by yourself without a team, please go on to "Step Three.")

Place your scores in the column below marked, "Individual Score."

Then, discuss each person's individual scores, reach consensus* as a team on each of the 20 questions and place those scores in column marked, "TEAM SCORE." (35 min.)

(Before starting the discussion, make sure everyone reads "Guidelines for Reaching Consensus" on page 7 for a mutual understanding of what consensus is.)

QUESTIONS:	INDIVIDUAL SCORE	TEAM SCORE
#1		
#2		
#3		
#4		
#5		
#6		
#7		
#8		
#9		
#10		
#11		
#12		
#13		
#14		
#15		
#16		
#17		
#18		
#19		
#20		

*Guidelines for Reaching Consensus:

1. Make sure everyone is heard from and feels listened to.
2. Do not vote—your aim is to talk through the issue until you've reached an agreement everyone can support.
3. Consensus may not mean that you are in 100% agreement, but you've been heard and you'll support the team's decision.
4. Do not give in just to reach agreement—view conflict and differences of opinion as good.
5. Be open. Strive for a creative solution.
6. Ask questions and make sure you understand everyone's opinion before you make up your mind.

Step Three- Interpreting Your Scores

Total Your *Individual* Scores For: Total Your *Team* Scores For:

Question #1: _____   #1: _____
Question #3: _____   #3: _____

    Total: [   ]   Total: [   ]

These questions reflect the amount of "Information/Communication" received. If the totals are less than "10," more information and communication is needed for increased empowerment.

Total Your *Individual* Scores For: Total Your *Team* Scores For:

Question #2: _____   #2: _____
Question #4: _____   #4: _____
Question #5: _____   #5: _____

    Total: [   ]   Total: [   ]

These questions reflect the amount of "Training/Skills" received. If the totals are less than "15," more training/skills are needed for increased empowerment.

Total Your *Individual* Scores For:

Question #6: _____
Question #7: _____
Question #8: _____
Question #10: _____
Question #11: _____
Question #12: _____
Question #13: _____
Question #14: _____
Question #15: _____
Question #16: _____
Question #17: _____

Total: [____]

Total Your *Team* Scores For:

#6: _____
#7: _____
#8: _____
#10: _____
#11: _____
#12: _____
#13: _____
#14: _____
#15: _____
#16: _____
#17: _____

Total: [____]

These questions reflect "Decision-Making Power." If the totals are less than "55," more decision-making power is needed (but only after information and training has been received).

Total Your *Individual* Scores For:

Question #9: _____
Question #18: _____
Question #19: _____
Question #20: _____

Total: [____]

Total Your *Team* Scores For:

#9: _____
#18: _____
#19: _____
#20: _____

Total: [____]

These questions reflect "Motivation & Rewards." If the totals are less than "20," more is needed in the areas of motivation and reward.

Step Four- Individual Exercise

After interpreting your individual/team scores, write "actions" that will increase your empowerment. (5 min.)

• Individual actions I need to take to increase my empowerment at work:

_____

_____

_____

_____

_____

Step Five- Team Exercise

As a total team discuss and reach consensus* on the actions needed to increase the team's empowerment: (15 min.)

_____

_____

_____

_____

_____

*See "*Guidelines for Reaching Consensus*" on page 7.

EMPOWERMENT: A DEFINITION

If everyone agrees that empowerment is desirable, even critical, why is it so difficult to achieve? Part of the problem is a failure to define what it really means on a day-to-day basis. In order to make empowerment a reality, everyone in the organization needs to understand and agree on what it means currently and what it will mean in the future.

The following is our definition of what empowered people and organizations actually do:

"Real" Empowerment Is-

- **Providing people throughout the organization with communication and information on all aspects of their work and the *total* business.** You can't expect people to take responsibility until they know the facts. Empowered people need information on costs, quality standards, customers, vendors/suppliers, competitors, budgets, etc.

- **Constantly training/educating people**
  - *Technical Training* - to become better at their work and learn new skills (cross-training for multiple skills, quality, and safety training)
  - *Interpersonal/Team Training* - to become better at working with one another to achieve high-performance (communication, team development, effective meetings, conflict management, leadership skills, decision-making, problem-solving, etc.)

  - *Administrative Skills Training* - to be able to do the administrative duties that traditional supervision used to do (scheduling, budgeting, interviewing, etc.)

- **Having decision-making power**
  After receiving information and skills training, people should be empowered to make decisions concerning their work. Delegating too soon is really "dumping." People need to be empowered over time. It's wise to begin with easier decisions at first, and then delegate the more difficult ones later, after people have had some experience with making decisions and taking responsibility for consequences. There is no limit to what empowered people and teams can do. High-performing teams make decisions on vacation scheduling, work scheduling, overtime, training, hiring and firing team members, peer appraisal, etc. But to turn this over all at once would overwhelm a team, instead, this should take place over a period of years.

- **Being able to measure and being rewarded for results**
  Key measures are usually: quantity, quality, service, etc. After measuring, empowered people and teams analyze the measures and figure out how to improve (self-correct). For "smartening" the work, empowered people are recognized and rewarded for their performance as individuals, teams, sites, business units, etc. Rewards tied to performance (pay-for-skills, gainsharing, lump sum bonus, profit-sharing, etc.) create a win-win for the employee and the organization.

QUESTIONS:

- How is your organization defining "empowerment?"

_____

_____

_____

- Does this definition enable people to know what *to do* differently?

. . . the average worker? _____

_____

. . . supervisors/team leaders? _____

_____

. . . managers? _____

_____

. . . support people? _____

_____

. . . others? _____

_____

BARRIERS TO "REAL" EMPOWERMENT

BARRIERS TO INFORMATION/ COMMUNICATION:

- inadequate information systems
- people hoarding information
- functional "fiefdoms"
- only giving information on a "need to know" basis
- not valuing the importance of communication
- seeing meetings as a "waste of time"
- not having the proper vehicles: bulletin boards, newsletters, etc.
- not sharing information with front-line people
- organization structure that blocks communication and information from flowing up, down, or sideways (and when it does flow, it's slow and often distorted)

BARRIERS TO TRAINING/ SKILLS:

- enough time
- enough money
- not believing that everyone needs training
- not giving training the organizational support and commitment needed to be effective
- not redesigning the system to incorporate the new skills/training
- not rewarding people for learning
- not having enough people to fill-in while others train
- viewing training as an expense rather than an investment

BARRIERS TO SHARING DECISION-MAKING POWER:

- leaders not wanting to share power
- leaders lacking delegation and coaching skills
- fear of letting-go
- fear of chaos and lack of control
- self-fulfilling prophecy that workers are incapable of making good decisions
- lacking patience for time required for team decision-making
- fear of mistakes
- belief that people would rather be "told what to do"
- not believing a team can make a better decision than an individual
- wanting to hold on to power and control
- fear of losing job if subordinates take over decision-making power
- believing the traditional bureaucratic way is best
- believing only some people are capable of making good decisions
- organizational design that allows no forum for people to come together and make decisions
- ineffective meetings where one person calls all the shots
- autocratic management
- caste system

BARRIERS TO MOTIVATION & REWARDS:

- treating rewards as a "taboo" subject
- not understanding that security, social, and growth needs *all* influence motivation
- not understanding what motivation is all about
- believing money is *not* a motivator (even when tied to performance)
- believing motivation is something you either have or you don't have
- not understanding how organization culture influences motivation
- not understanding how leadership style influences motivation

- not understanding that rewards tied to performance create a win-win between the needs of people and the needs of the organization
- not seeing motivation as the *key* job of leadership
- not understanding that work redesign/reengineering must tap human motivation in order to succeed
- not understanding the critical link between motivation and performance
- not appreciating that motivated people are the key to high-performing organizations

TYPES OF EMPLOYEE INVOLVEMENT
& DEGREE OF EMPOWERMENT

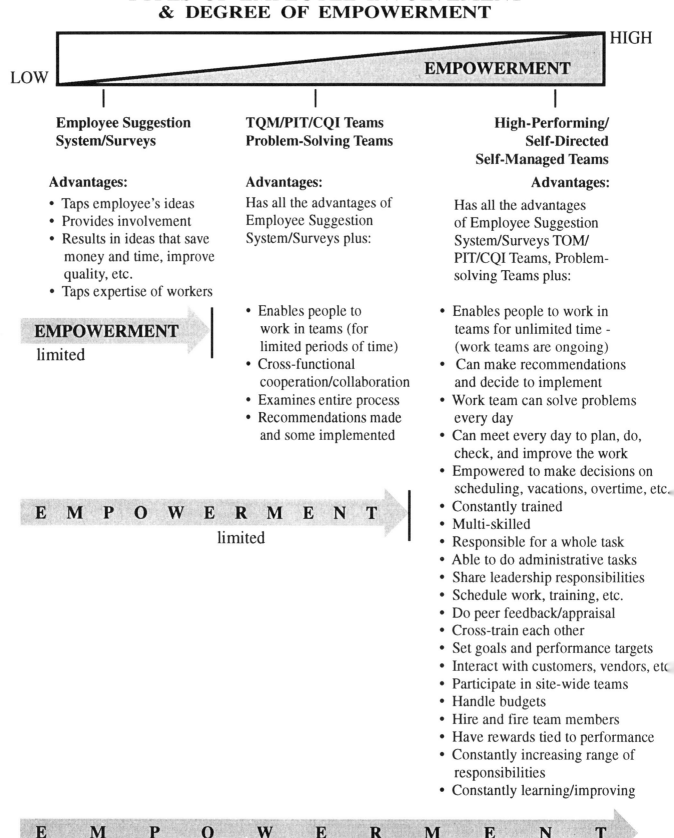

Employee Suggestion System/Surveys	TQM/PIT/CQI Teams Problem-Solving Teams	High-Performing/ Self-Directed Self-Managed Teams

Advantages:

- Taps employee's ideas
- Provides involvement
- Results in ideas that save money and time, improve quality, etc.
- Taps expertise of workers

Advantages:

Has all the advantages of Employee Suggestion System/Surveys plus:

- Enables people to work in teams (for limited periods of time)
- Cross-functional cooperation/collaboration
- Examines entire process
- Recommendations made and some implemented

Advantages:

Has all the advantages of Employee Suggestion System/Surveys TOM/ PIT/CQI Teams, Problem-solving Teams plus:

- Enables people to work in teams for unlimited time - (work teams are ongoing)
- Can make recommendations and decide to implement
- Work team can solve problems every day
- Can meet every day to plan, do, check, and improve the work
- Empowered to make decisions on scheduling, vacations, overtime, etc.
- Constantly trained
- Multi-skilled
- Responsible for a whole task
- Able to do administrative tasks
- Share leadership responsibilities
- Schedule work, training, etc.
- Do peer feedback/appraisal
- Cross-train each other
- Set goals and performance targets
- Interact with customers, vendors, etc
- Participate in site-wide teams
- Handle budgets
- Hire and fire team members
- Have rewards tied to performance
- Constantly increasing range of responsibilities
- Constantly learning/improving

EMPOWERMENT limited

E M P O W E R M E N T limited

E M P O W E R M E N T unlimited

All employee involvement efforts are based on empowering employees by tapping their ideas, suggestions, and expertise. But by their very nature some are very limited forms of involvement.

EMPLOYEE SUGGESTION SYSTEMS/ SURVEYS: Limited to having employees submit their opinions/ideas/suggestions/recommendations which are then examined and, if approved, implemented.

TQM TEAMS/PROBLEM-SOLVING TEAMS/PROCESS IMPROVEMENT TEAMS: Give employees more empowerment than mere suggestions systems or surveys. Now, people from various functions and departments meet face-to-face periodically to pool their knowledge of how the whole system works and together make suggestions, recommendations, problem-solve, examine and analyze processes, and procedures. This collaboration taps creativity and creates synergy. These teams may be able to implement some of their own ideas and others will be recommendations for higher level management to consider.

HIGH-PERFORMANCE/SELF-DIRECTED/SELF-MANAGED WORK TEAMS: These terms are all different names for the same type of team. Empowerment on these work teams is a never-ending process because as the team receives more and more information and training, their capabilities and decision-making power increases. Ideally, these teams have no limit on what they're capable of doing—over time.

A mature team (more than two years old) would be able to not just make suggestions, but implement improvements on a daily basis, problem-solve, check their own quality, set goals and measure against performance targets, interact directly with customers, vendors, and suppliers, represent the team at outside meetings, share team leadership, do peer review, cross-train to become multi-skilled, and make important decisions (i.e., vacation scheduling, overtime, hiring and firing). Interest in self-direction has grown steadily over the last few years because companies that have self-directed work teams find the results can be astonishing: higher quality, lower costs, flatter structures, faster service to customers, more flexibility, higher morale and worker satisfaction. Many organizations are trying to evolve their other employee involvement efforts (quality/problem-solving teams) into self-directed work teams. Other organizations redesign/reengineer focusing on core processes peopled by self-directed teams as the basic organizational building block.

We feel that all these types of employee involvement are needed. Ultimately, we think self-directed teams should be the aim of organizations. But, we also want to stress that implementing successful SDWTs means changing organizational systems and structures (not the case with other forms of employee involvement) and unless time for training is given to the teams, they won't reach their full potential.

BARRIERS TO BUILDING HIGH-PERFORMING TEAMS

If high-performing/self-directed/self-managed teams are so great, why don't all organizations have them? The answer is twofold: Not all organizations want to take empowerment as far as self-direction and not all are successful in implementing and maintaining their teams because of the many barriers, as well as, the time and effort involved.

The following is a list of barriers that hinder teams from reaching their full potential:

- lack of trust
- a climate of fear
- not involving *all* the key stakeholders
- not involving the Union (forming a "Partnership")
- lack of top leadership commitment
  - changing leaders too frequently
  - not really understanding the concept:
    —not "walking the talk"
    —not providing the resources needed (time & money)
    —not developing new vision, mission, and values
    —not leading the effort (delegating to others)
- insufficient time to change
  - short term goals & measures
  - expecting a "Quick-Fix"

- resistance from:
  - supervisors
  - managers
  - support people
  - union
  - workers
- insufficient training
- systems & structures not designed to support teams
- failure to redefine the role of leadership
- leaders not "letting go"
- too little or too much structure
- no transition plan
- not providing work security assurance
- not communicating what's happening
- treating change like a "program" not a process
- overwhelming the team members (too much responsibility and decision-making power before the they've had training)
- a history not conducive to employee involvement
- not educating everyone in the work place about high-performance/self-direction
- not understanding that this is a *total* cultural transformation

Despite the length of this list, we feel these barriers can, should, and must be overcome because the potential of teams is enormous.

HIGH-INVOLVEMENT EXERCISE

Identifying & Overcoming Barriers

Learning Objective: To help individuals and groups identify organizational barriers and determine actions for overcoming them.

Directions:

Step One- Individual Exercise

Which of the barriers described in this section exist in your organization? (5 min.)

_____   _____

_____   _____

_____   _____

_____   _____

_____   _____

Step Two- Team Exercise

Discuss the individual answers to "Step One" and reach consensus* on the following:

What are *5 actions* needed to overcome these barriers? (25 min.)

1. _____

2. _____

3. _____

4. _____

5. _____

*See "*Guidelines for Reaching Consensus*" on page 7.

NOTES:

ACTION TWO

Changing the "Total" Culture

- *Why We Have to Change Our Traditional Organizations to High-Performance Models*

- *The Shape of a High-Performance Organization*

- *High-Involvement Exercise: Dealing with Resistance to Change*

- *State-of-Mind Shift for "Real" Empowerment*

- *High-Involvement Exercise: Questions People Need to Have Answered During Change*

- *Overcoming Barriers to Change: Our Experience*

- *Helping People Move Through the "Stages of Change"*
  - *Questions*
  - *Actions for Helping People Change*

WHY WE HAVE TO CHANGE OUR TRADITIONAL ORGANIZATIONS TO HIGH-PERFORMANCE MODELS

For two-hundred years most companies have been organized in the traditional bureaucratic, pyramidal structure.

This system is finally changing because its weaknesses are proving to be costly, and even fatal. Some major flaws of traditional, hierarchical organizations are that they're:

- **TOO SLOW** It takes too long for communication/information to go up, down, and sideways. Work waits in functional silos instead of being expedited by process-driven, whole systems.

- **NOT CUSTOMER-DRIVEN** It often ignores the whole purpose of an organization, which is to serve customers.

- **REWARDS NOT TIED TO PERFORMANCE** Only top 5 to 10% receive bonuses (and these are not always tied to performance).

- **WASTEFUL** It separates "thinkers" from "doers" and quality suffers. Too many people are checking the work of others and catching mistakes after they're made, causing expensive, time-consuming rework.

- **CONTROL MODEL** Designed to control people rather than utilize & maximize their potential.

TRADITIONAL "DIRECT AND CONTROL" MODEL

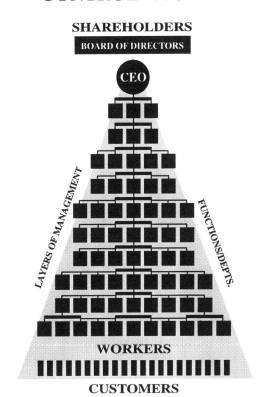

- **NOT RESPONSIVE TO CHANGING CUSTOMER & MARKET DEMANDS** Designed to respond to your boss rather than to customers & market demands.

- **FEAR-DRIVEN** Organization held together by subtle and not-so-subtle fear.

- **NOT MOTIVATING** The traditional organization has too many narrow, dull, fragmented jobs, especially at the bottom of the organization. To be successful today, organizations need highly trained, multi-skilled, flexible, empowered workers who are motivated to constantly learn and improve everything.

"HIGH PERFORMANCE" MODEL

Fast, flexible, and customer-driven—high-performance organizations have various names (i.e., horizontal or nuclear organization) and various shapes (i.e., network, lattice, concentric circles), but they all have the following characteristics:

CUSTOMERS ARE ON TOP What the customer wants and says drives the company. Everyone listens to the customer's definition of quality and strives to meet or exceed expectations.

WORK TEAMS ARE DESIGNED AROUND CORE PROCESSES Empowered teams do what is needed to meet constantly changing customer and market demands.

LEADERS KNOW HOW TO SUPPORT TEAMS Coaching, counseling, training, removing barriers, providing resources, and listening to the team members and customers are some of the new roles for participative leaders.

CEO SEES ROLE AS LEADING THE ORGANIZATION INTO THE FUTURE High-performance organizations need leaders that know how to empower teams by passing down business information, constantly providing time and money for training, and making sure people are rewarded for their performance. Letting the teams take care of the day-to-day work, frees top management to make long-range strategic plans.

VALUES-DRIVEN Believing that human beings are capable of controlling themselves when given information, training, responsibility, and rewards.

THE SHAPE OF A HIGH-PERFORMANCE ORGANIZATION

- **FLAT** As few layers as possible between the work teams (who do the work; plan it; schedule it; build-in quality; make decisions) and top management
- **EMPOWERED WORK TEAMS** designed around core work processes, not functions or departments
- **INFORMATION** is provided directly to the teams so they can make sound day-to-day decisions and management can focus on removing barriers, supporting teams, listening to customers, and making long-range plans.
- **FAST** Decisions are made quickly by multi-skilled, flexible teams who can customize high-quality products at the lowest possible cost.
- **CONTINUOUS IMPROVEMENT** Everyone is constantly working on improving something every day, so change is constant.
- **CUSTOMER-DRIVEN** Everyone is listening to customers (in a variety of ways: face-to-face, over the telephone, written feedback, etc.) and acting on what they hear.
- **QUALITY** is defined by the customer and is everyone's responsibility.
- **CONSTANT TRAINING & LEARNING** People are seen as the most valuable resource the company has. Investing in every employee is a core value and providing training and learning opportunities shows the importance of people as an appreciating asset.
- **CHANGE AS A PROCESS** - A permanent change in state-of-mind, culture, and way of doing business—not a "program" that has a beginning and ending. *Everyone's* job will change as the organization evolves.
- **PARTNERSHIPS** with unions, vendors, suppliers, and customers.
- **REWARDS TIED TO PERFORMANCE** Teams set performance targets, measure quality, quantity, customer service, etc. and are rewarded for results.

The hardest part of creating successful high-performing teams is having the right "state of mind." The changes we're talking about require learning a different set of attitudes.

"State-of-Mind" Shift
From Traditional To High Performance

Traditional	High Performance
Many Levels	Flat Organization
Autocratic Style	Participative Style
Directive Decision-making (1 person decides)	Consensus Decision-making (the group decides)
Competitive	Cooperative
"Tell me what to do"	"How can *we* work smarter?"
"It's only a job"	"It's my job"
Skilled in one job	Multi-Skilled
Low Risk-taking	Innovative
Reacting to Change	Seizing Opportunities
Stability & Predictability	Constant Change
Management and Union as Adversaries (Win-Lose)	Management and Union as Partners (Win-Win)
Internal Organization Driven	Customer Driven
Rules Bound & Slow	Flexible & Fast
Doing Things Right	Doing the "Right" Things
"I only work here"	"I am the company"
Power Over Workers (Told what to do)	Empowered Work Force (Able to do what is right)
"If it's not broken, don't fix it"	Constantly Learning & Improving
Acceptable Quality & Service	World-Class Quality & Service
Technology First	People First
People as Spare Parts	People as Valuable Resources
Control of Supervisor	Commitment of Teams
Procedures Book	Self-Control

HIGH-INVOLVEMENT EXERCISE:

Dealing With Resistance to Change

Learning Objective:

To help people identify the nature of the resistance to change and involve people in discussing problems and developing strategies for turning resistance into commitment.

Directions:

Step One- Individual Exercise

As you read the following thirteen reasons people resist change, circle what you believe are the top 4 reasons why the people in your organization are resisting change. These do *not* have to be in order of priority. (5 min.)

Reasons People Resist Change:

1- CONCERN FOR JOB SECURITY

2- LOSS OF CONTROL

3- TOO MUCH AMBIGUITY/UNCERTAINTY

4- LACK OF CLEAR GOALS & DIRECTION

5- NEW THINGS MEAN MORE WORK

6- NOT WANTING TO CHANGE HABITS

7- FEELING LEFT OUT OF CHANGE PROCESS

8- LACK OF NEW SKILLS NEEDED

9- NO TRANSITION PLAN IN PLACE

10- LACK OF TRUST IN LEADERSHIP

11- LACK OF AGREEMENT ON WHAT SHOULD CHANGE

12- NEED TIME TO ADJUST

13- TOO MANY CHANGES GOING ON AT THE SAME TIME

Step Two- Team Exercise

After everyone in the group has circled their top 4 reasons, ask for a show of hands on each item. As a facilitator reads each item out loud, have everyone who circled that item as one of their four, raise their hands. Count the number of hands to determine which are the team's top four. (5 min.)

Step Three- Team Exercise

Read back the top four reasons the group chose and have an open discussion. (5 min.)

Step Four- Team Exercise

Brainstorm* all the actions that could turn this resistance into commitment. (First, read the "Guidelines for Brainstorming" below.) Choose a facilitator to write the group's list on flip chart paper as people call out their actions.

---

*Guidelines for Brainstorming:

1. Call out anything that pops into your mind.
2. Put everything said on a flip chart (if something is repeated add it also).
3. No discussion (at this time).
4. No judgment.
5. Silence is O.K. (just wait patiently without saying anything and more ideas might come forth).
6. Adding ideas onto other people's ideas is fine and should be encouraged.
7. Be creative (anything goes).
8. Have fun!

ACTIONS FOR TURNING RESISTANCE INTO COMMITMENT

_____   _____

_____   _____

_____   _____

_____   _____

Step Five- Team Exercise

Compare the group's list with the one below. Our experience has been that these actions really make a difference. Remember, resistance is a natural response to change. How you deal with resistance is what matters. Some of the strongest "resisters" can turn into the most committed advocates if these things are done:

- Involvement Builds Commitment!
  Involve as many people as possible. Create opportunities for everyone to participate in the change process.
- Communicate
  Let people know what's happening so there are no surprises.
- Create a Transition Plan
  Break big changes into small, manageable steps so people/teams don't feel overwhelmed.
- Train
  People need to feel competent with new skills and attitudes before they can change.

- "Walk-the-Talk"
  Actions speak louder than words. Role model the new behavior.
- Build Trust
- Keep Promises
- Share the Pain
  Don't ask one group to make all the sacrifices.
- Reward & Recognize Effort
- Listen
- Don't "Shoot the Messenger"
- Don't Punish Mistakes
  Encourage risk-taking and learning from mistakes
- Provide Time & Resources
- Realize Everyone's Role Will Change
- Provide Information & Answer Questions
- Dialogue
  Provide forums (large meetings, small sessions, town meetings, task forces, committees, study groups, etc.) where people can express their concerns and problem-solve together
- Have patience
  Don't expect committment to happen overnight; it has to grow.

HIGH-INVOLVEMENT EXERCISE:

Questions People Need To Have Answered During Change

Learning Objective:

At each stage of change (before, during, and after implementation), certain questions need to be discussed and answered. The purpose of this exercise is to create a dialogue about these questions to give people an opportunity to voice concerns, fears, hopes, etc.

Directions:

Step One- Individual Exercise

Answer the following questions: (If you don't know the answer to a question, leave it blank.) (10 min.)

1. Why are we doing this? What is the compelling reason/s driving this change?

_____

_____

_____

2. Is it important that we do this? What might happen if we don't?

_____

_____

_____

3. Is this change *doable?*

_____

_____

_____

4. What am I supposed to do?

    _____

    _____

    _____

5. What are my goals, objectives, etc.?

    _____

    _____

    _____

6. How will the organization benefit?

    _____

    _____

    _____

7. How will I benefit?

    _____

    _____

    _____

8. How will this team benefit?

    _____

    _____

    _____

9. How am I doing? (Is there feedback provided to me on how well I'm doing or what mistakes I'm making?)

    _____

    _____

    _____

• How are we doing as a team?

_____

_____

_____

10. Is support available?

_____

_____

_____

11. Have I received enough training?

_____

_____

_____

• Has the team received enough training? (Technical? Interpersonal? Administrative?)

_____

_____

_____

12. What do I see as the "barriers" to this change being successful?

_____

_____

_____

13. What needs to be done to overcome these barriers?

_____

_____

_____

14. What happens if I make a mistake?

_____

_____

_____

15. What are we going to be like when the change has taken place? (Is the vision/mission clear to people?)

_____

_____

_____

16. Other concerns I have?

_____

_____

• Other concerns the Team has?

_____

_____

Step Two- Team Exercise

After everyone has finished answering the questions, discuss and reach consensus*
on each one. (35 min.)
*See "*Guidelines for Reaching Consensus,*" on page 7.

OVERCOMING BARRIERS TO CHANGE:
OUR EXPERIENCE

- The key to successful change efforts is employee involvement. People tend to support change when they have played a part in shaping it. If changes are imposed on people, they resist.

- The vast majority of people are successful in adapting to these new workplaces. Many people, especially frontline workers, feel that high-performance is just common sense and they welcome the changes.

- A few people will probably be unwilling to change and they may choose to leave. If that's not possible, there will always be individual contributor jobs as technical experts to many teams.

- The higher up in the organization one goes; the more difficult it is to change. This is true for several reasons: Executives, managers, and supervisors see more to lose than to gain in making these changes (at least at first). Also, traditional perks are removed, power shifts, and roles drastically change.

- Eventually, there is a sense of gain, but this takes time and patience. All the training and learning that takes place slows things down at first and doesn't pay off for quite some time. When it does, leaders find that they are now free to do many things they always wanted to do to make the organization more effective.

- In order for any change effort to succeed it must be viewed as an on-going process and not just a "quick-fix" "program-of-the-month." It is up to top management to prove they are committed before anyone else will take change seriously.

- Since there are now fewer layers, alternate career paths need to be created so everyone gets a sense of growth without necessarily being promoted to another level. And since there will be fewer supervisors and managers, people need to be rewarded without going into management, so redesigning reward systems becomes important.

- Everyone needs assurances that productivity gains will not cost them their jobs. Unless this is stated, people will drag their feet and even hold back ideas that put them at risk. It's a lose-lose for the organization and the employees.

- Successful change is about building partnerships with employees, unions, customers, vendors, and suppliers.

- Changing traditional organizations means TOTAL cultural transformation. Changing just a part won't work; it has to be the *whole* system.

THE FOUR STAGES OF CHANGE

Changing traditional organizations to high-performance models means "unlearning" almost everything we've been taught about how organizations operate. This means dramatic changes for human beings and, let's face it, we usually don't like change! It's more work (especially, at first). We're afraid of making mistakes. We'll need to learn new skills. And we don't like all the uncertainty. Change takes time and we need to be patient with ourselves and others because we don't all change at the same rate.

The research on change says we go through four stages:

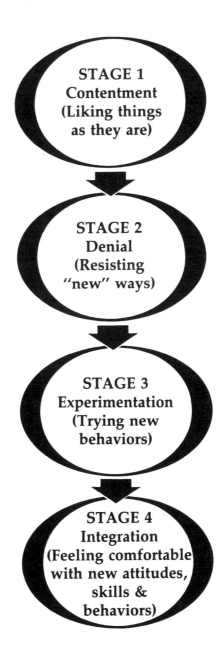

QUESTIONS: ?...?...?...?...?

After reading about the "Four Stages of Change," answer the following questions: (10 min.)

1. Which stage best describes where you are at this time? (Explain your choice.)

_____

_____

_____

_____

2. At which stage do you think most team members are? (Explain your choice.)

_____

_____

_____

_____

3. At which stage do you think most managers/supervisors are? (Explain your choice.)

_____

_____

_____

_____

ACTIONS FOR HELPING PEOPLE CHANGE

■ Providing Information On:
  • Vision
  • Mission
  • Goals
  • State-of-the-Business
  • Support/Training/Resources Available
  • Other High-Performance Organizations

■ Answering Important Questions:
  • Why are we doing this?
  • What's in it for me?
  • What's going to happen to me and my job?

■ Listening (to words & feelings)

■ Not Judging

■ Giving Positive Reinforcement

■ Role-Modeling New Behaviors

■ Coaching/Counseling/Teaching/Training

■ Being Patient

■ Encouraging Risk-taking

■ Not "Shooting the Messenger"

■ Providing Resources

■ Removing Barriers

■ Creating Two-Way Communication Forums

■ Involving Instead of "Selling"

NOTES:

A C T I O N THREE

Leadership That "Walks-the-Talk"

- *Reasons Top Leadership Resists Leading Change Efforts*
- *Top Leadership's "New" Role*
- *High-Involvement Exercise*
- *Exerting Influence*
- *Site Visit Questionnaire*

THE NUMBER ONE BARRIER TO THE SUCCESS OF CHANGE EFFORTS

"The real tragedy of corporate life is that changes occur only after it's too late. Instead of capitalizing on opportunity, these companies are responding to crisis. And when you're down, it's pretty hard to put Humpty Dumpty back together again." James O'Toole, Dir., Univ. Of So. California's Leadership Institute (Business Week: Feb. 15, 1993)

The above quote from an article entitled, "Requiem for Yesterday's CEO: Old-Style Execs Who Can't Adapt Are Losing Their Hold," sums up the crisis facing American organizations today. Based on our experience the number one barrier to succeeding with change efforts is top management's lack of understanding that their personal involvement is essential. Leading an organization into the future is not a job that can be delegated.

Sadly, most leaders "talk it" and use all the right buzz words, but they don't "walk it," in fact, their behavior sends an opposite message. By not getting directly involved in steering committees or quality councils, they are telling everyone that they have other, more important matters to spend their time on. Why then should anyone else take it seriously? This scenario is the main reason change "programs" come and go in American organizations without successfully changing the total culture.

Leader's don't seem to appreciate that people are watching and listening to what they "DO," not what they "SAY." The old cliche that "actions speak louder than words" is very true when it comes to change efforts. In order to change, people need role models and that is what top leadership should provide, but rarely does. Leaders who succeed at transforming their organizations (and there are some) change themselves. They spend less time on speeches and slogans and more time with people, listening to frontline workers, leading steering committees/quality councils, and learning new skills and attitudes.

In this section we're going to focus on three key points:

- Why top leadership often delegates the leadership of change.
- What top leadership's role should be.
- What can be done to convince leaders that their role must change if the organization is going to change.

REASONS TOP LEADERSHIP RESISTS LEADING CHANGE EFFORTS:

- See their job as primarily managing assets
- Tend to be focused on and rewarded for short-term results
- Tend to be "doers" not learners & don't keep abreast of newest information on how to manage organizations
- Not likely to lead a change effort that goes against the core beliefs of the system that promoted them

- Lack knowledge of what to do
- Don't see it as their number one priority
- Often delegate the task to others
- Don't want to change themselves (attitudes, behaviors, values, etc.)
- Don't see themselves as part of the problem
- Don't want to take a risk on unproven theories
- Find it easier to maintain the status quo
- May not be with the company long enough to invest in a long term process
- Don't know how to redesign/reengineer an organization
- Don't want to "unlearn" the skills & attitudes they've mastered and learn new ones
- Lack the values/attitudes/assumptions needed for high-performance
- Don't understand human motivation
- Reluctant to let go of power/control/status
- Don't want to share decision-making power
- Not accustomed to working in teams
- Don't understand that their behavior is what influences others, not speeches, or slogans
- Say they want change, but are unwilling to change measures, systems, etc.
- Want everyone else to change
- Want employee commitment, but won't give job security assurance
- Want proof that something works before they'll try it and by then it's too late
- Don't understand that quality, commitment, & high-performance can't be dictated
- Lack appreciation for the importance of participation & involvement
- Don't know they don't know
- Find it difficult to set aside self-interest and focus on what's best for the organization
- Have never experienced a high-performance organization
- Want to be able to make quick decisions (lack the patience required for consensus)
- Would rather "sell" than involve
- Don't see their primary role as that of change agent leading the organization into a new, uncharted future
- Aren't comfortable with ambiguity

TOP LEADERSHIP'S *NEW* ROLE

If the leadership of American organizations is going to succeed in turning dinosaurs into high-performing organizations, they're going to have to do the following types of activities:

■ Lead the organization into the future by:
  • Educating themselves
    —reading books
    —attending workshops/conferences
    —networking with others
    —benchmarking with innovative companies
    —visiting sites
  • Examining their own assumptions about organizations, people, and performance (i.e. having others fear you)
  • Listening to the people of the organization, "walking-the-floor," and being accessible
■ Set overall direction by determining:
    —What business are we in?
    —Who are our customers?
    —What is our competitive advantage?
    —How can we maximize this advantage?
  • Set long term goals and not settling for the "quick fix".
  • Set high expectations

• Form a steering committee made of representatives of *all* key stakeholders who together:
    —examine the current environment
    —assess the current culture
    —plan the future
    —decide how to transition
    —create the new vision/mission/values/goals
    —decide how to move forward
■ Communicate (speeches & two-way dialogues)
■ Involve everyone in the organization
  • Providing the necessary resources
    —information
    —time
    —money
    —training
■ Listen, learn, have faith, have patience, be willing to change
■ Monitor the change effort by:
  • providing two-way communication forums
  • viewing conflict as positive
  • not "shooting the messenger" (encouraging upward communication)
  • providing more business information to everyone
  • increasing ownership of business results
  • making sure people know what they need to do to impact the results

- making sure decisions are made by consensus
- focusing on the process (making sure it's participatory)
- changing behaviors by changing the organization's:
  —structure
  —measurement system
  —appraisal system
  —reward system
  —decision-making processes
  —information systems
  —leadership (from autocratic to participative)
- making sure employee ideas/ suggestions are listened to and implemented
- providing training for high-performance (and participating in it)
- asking questions & expecting informed answers
- building trust
- instituting study groups, task forces, problem-solving teams, process improvement teams, etc.
- forming an executive team
- rejecting hierarchical status symbols and eliminating all discriminators
- getting involved with customers
- being accessible ("walking-the-floor" and listening to employees)
- recognizing and rewarding the new attitudes and behaviors

■ Create something new and better not just "reorganizing" what exists

■ Inspire people by being a role model of the new attitudes and behaviors

■ Provide learning opportunities for everyone

■ Push-down decisions to the people that should be making them

■ Be part of a leadership team

■ Be more interested in the organization than in personal gain

■ Model sacrifice (i.e., at Nucor Steel "pain starts at the top")

■ Be totally open and honest

■ Build trust; drive out fear

■ Realize people manage themselves, but leaders manage the context that allows change to happen

■ Create a "win-win" for the employees and the organization

■ Demonstrate customer-focus

■ Be proactive

■ See change as the real job any leader

■ Believe change must start with oneself

HIGH-INVOLVEMENT EXERCISE:

Top Management's New Role

Learning Objective:

To discuss and agree on the actions top management should *stop* and *start* doing.

Directions:

Step One- Individual Exercise

List the actions you'd like top management to STOP DOING or START DOING. (5 min.)

_____

_____

_____

_____

_____

Step Two- Team Exercise

Discuss each person's list and reach consensus* on a team list of actions you'd like top management to STOP DOING or START DOING. (30 min.)

_____

_____

_____

_____

_____

_____

*See *"Guidelines for Reaching Consensus"* on page 7.

EXERTING INFLUENCE

We are often asked by the people we meet in our workshops, *"What can we do to encourage top management to lead these efforts?"*

Here are some behaviors that we have seen influence senior managers:

- Give them books to read
- Show them video documentaries of high-performance workplaces
- Invite them to a workshop/conference where they can learn new things and network with people from other organizations who are at various stages of change
- Benchmark with other companies in the same and different industries and find innovative practices to share with top leadership
- Invite senior managers to visit other sites with you (in the same or different industries). While there, talk to the frontline people, ask questions, and see if there are any discernible differences in culture.
- Invite top management to an on-site workshop you've sponsored where consultants will speak or conduct training
- Share data (research, surveys, assessments, etc.)
- Invite top leadership to participate on the Steering Committee and make a strong case why they *must* be on it if it is to succeed
- Have a group of people who've attended a workshop make a presentation on what they learned and actions they now recommend
- Have task forces/design teams present what they think needs to happen in order for change to be successful
- Never stop managing up. The most important thing you can do is involve your boss. Make sure he/she understands why change is needed and how important their support is (or they'll become a barrier).
- Consider succession planning. Discuss what might happen if your leadership changes. Take steps to insure the change effort will continue even when leaders change. (Example: Make it known that a committee will select the next leader based on the candidate's knowledge of and support for the changes taking place.) A good succession plan lets everyone know that this change effort has commitment and does not depend on any one sponsor.
- Do not allow fear of your manager or upper management stop you from saying or doing what's right.

Since site visits are so helpful to change efforts, we've devised this questionnaire for getting the most information out of your visit. (Tip: Make sure you speak directly with frontline people and not just official spokespeople.)

SITE VISIT QUESTIONNAIRE

Name of Site _____

Location _____

Contact Name _____

Description of Site _____

---

1. What was the nature of the change effort? (TQM? Self-Directed Teams? PITs? CQI? High-Performance? Other?)

    _____

2. What were the reasons driving the change? _____

    _____

3. When did the change begin? _____

4. Who was the sponsor? _____

5. Was there a Steering Committee? _____

    •   Design Team? _____

    •   Pilot/s? _____

6. What were the barriers/problems encountered during implementation?

    _____

    How were they handled? _____

    _____

7. What training was provided prior to implementation? _____

    _____

. . . since implementation? _____

_____

8. What was the time frame for the change effort? _____

_____

9. How were the changes communicated to the rest of the organization?

_____

10. How were others involved in the process:

    managers? _____

    supervisors? _____

    workers? _____

    support people? _____

    union? _____

11. What have been the results? (benefits & drawbacks) _____

_____

_____

_____

12. Is there a transition plan in place? How many years does it cover?

_____

13. Was the work redesigned/reengineered? _____

14. How is leadership currently handled:

    Do teams have an appointed leader? _____

    _____

    . . . a rotating leader? _____

    What is the new role for supervisors? _____

    . . . for managers? _____

15. If there are high-performing teams, what are they called? _____

    What do they do? _____

    _____

    What kinds of decisions do they make? _____

    What are they responsible for? _____

16. Are there fewer layers of management than before? _____

17. Has the organization culture changed? _____

18. What is better about this new way? _____

    . . . worse? _____

19. Have the systems changed:

    measurement? _____

    appraisal? _____

    reward? _____

    career development? _____

20. What advice would you give to an organization just starting the journey?

    _____

    _____

    _____

    _____

    _____

NOTES:

ACTION FOUR

Creating a Roadmap for the Transition

A 5-Phase Change Model:

- *Phase I: Vision, Values, Driving Force*
- *Phase II: Communication & Involvement*
- *Phase III: Redesign*
- *Phase IV: Implementation*
- *Phase V: Assessment/Expansion/Continuous Learning*

Any change effort should begin with a lot of up-front thought, analysis, discussion, planning, and preparation. Too often we see failures result from the following causes:

• One person or a small group makes all the decisions and dictates to everyone else.

• The sponsor delegates the leadership of the effort to someone else, sending the people of the organization a mixed message, "I want *you* to focus on changing this organization, but my time is being spent on more important things."

• Management decides to remove all supervisors and let teams "self-manage" (providing little or no training and support)

• Management decides to arbitrarily designate teams without analyzing and redesigning/reengineering the work processes first

• Management decides to start an employee involvement effort, but they leave out key stakeholders (i.e., union leaders, supervisors, middle managers, support people) thereby, *insuring* resistance instead of support

• Not enough time spent on educating and training people in new attitudes and skills

• Teams formed, but no long-term transition plan created to let them know what they're expected to do/learn over time

A successful change effort is not a "quick-fix" program, but a continuous learning process. In order to be successful change has to be viewed as participatory. You may, in visiting sites, see a design you like, but avoid the impulse to impose this on the people in your organization. That's a "program" and it probably won't work for the following reasons:

• No two companies or organizations are alike. Design a plan that fits your organization and your people.

• Participation requires everyone's involvement and that means a unique design.

• You need everyone's ideas and expertise to develop a sound plan. No *one* person or even a small group can think of everything.

• People tend to resist what they're not involved in designing. Asking people to participate in the planning and implementation not only taps everyone's expertise, but it gets everyone's buy-in. Remember, even a good plan will only succeed if people are committed to carrying it out.

• If you dictate a plan, your actions will contradict the very things you're trying to accomplish.

WHERE DO YOU START?

The following 5-Phase Change Model is based on the socio-technical-systems approach which has been used successfully since the early 1950s. It provides structure while still being an involving/participatory process:

5-PHASE CHANGE MODEL

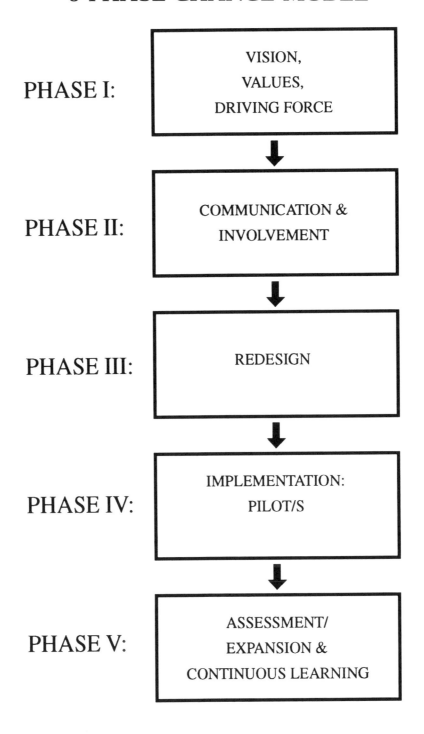

PHASE I:
VISION, VALUES,
DRIVING FORCE

- A sponsor initiates the need for change
  —This is usually top leadership (site manager or higher) who sees a problem that needs to be addressed or an opportunity to be capitalized (i.e., a new product/service, new site, etc.)

- A Steering Committee is formed, made-up of representatives of *all* the key stake-holders in the organization (across all functions/departments):
  —Managers
  —Supervisors
  —Workers
  —Union
  —Support People

(Size of group should try not to exceed 15 or consensus will be more difficult. This is true for all teams—Steering, Design, Pilots, and Work Teams.)

Purpose of Steering Committee:

- Assess the current environment outside the organization:
  —Market
  —Customers
  —Regulatory Agencies
  —Competition
  —Etc.

- Assess the environment inside the organization:
  —What business are we in?
  —Who are our customers?
  —What is our competitive advantage?
  —Are we currently organized to maximize our advantage?

- Determine what our core work processes are:
  —Analyze how the work is currently being done
    (the technical system)
  —Analyze how the people of the organization are affected by the organization culture (the social system). Are their talents, skills, knowledge, expertise, involvement, motivation being tapped?

- Determine how well the current organization meets the outside demands now and in the future (5, 10 or more years)

- If it's determined that a gap exists between how the organization is now and how it needs to be to maximize competitive advantage, consensus must be reached on a new organization culture based on new core values, vision, mission and philosophy.

- Decide what the next step will be. This might entail some or all of the following:
  —Reengineering work processes
  —Redesigning the present technical & social systems
  —Beginning employee involvement with temporary problem-solving, quality or process improvement teams

Activities of Steering Committee:

- Meet once a week for half or full day

- Team building training to enable the group to work together more effectively and to be the first "real" team. (This is often led by an outside consultant for objectivity and an inside consultant for continuity.)

- Educate themselves by:
  —Reading
  —Attending training sessions/workshops/conferences
  —Visiting sites
  —Benchmarking with other companies

- Reach consensus on:
  —Why we're changing? (driving force)
  —What we're changing to? (new vision, values)
  —Where and when change will begin?
  —Scope of change? (entire organization or part?)
    (If there's to be a pilot, where would be best?)

- Allocate resources

- Create a plan for communicating to everyone

- Create forums where everyone in the organization can dialogue (two-way communication) about their hopes and concerns

- Create a plan for involving everyone by giving them an opportunity to participate

- Choose representatives for Design Team/s

- Give Design Team a charter (boundaries, scope, mission, goals, etc. of redesign)

- Continue to meet periodically throughout the change effort to steer it, support it, and maintain it by making key decisions

- Publish meeting minutes and post them throughout the organization

PHASE II: COMMUNICATION & INVOLVEMENT

Lack of communication and involvement are the root causes of many change effort failures. People tend to resist what they do not understand (preventable by communication) and feel left out of (preventable by involvement).

Purpose of Phase II:

- Begin a two-way dialogue with everyone in the organization about the present, the future, the business, and the shape of the changes that need to take place. This communication should begin as soon as possible, therefore, Phases I and II overlap (as do all the phases). The Steering Committee should not be cloaked in secrecy. Everyone should know who is on it, what its purpose is, and what its activities are.

- Build commitment through communication and involvement. We're frequently asked, "How do you *sell* change?" We don't think "selling" is the way to bring about change. If you involve me and we create something together, you won't have to "sell" me on it and we can all focus our efforts on doing it.

Activities of Phase II:

- Communication sessions- (large meetings and small, informal sessions) where people can ask questions, raise concerns, voice feelings (fears, hopes, etc.)

- Post minutes of Steering Committee sessions

- Make sure everyone understands and reaches consensus on:
  —Why we're changing
  —What we're changing to
  —Why it will be worthwhile
  —What will happen to me and my job

- Create opportunities for:
  —Managers, supervisors, and workers to voice concerns over job security and changing roles and have input on shaping their new roles
  —Everyone to serve on task forces, committees, etc.
  —Educating everyone
    - Books, articles, videos
    - Training (workshops, conferences, cross-training, etc.)
      - Technical skills & "soft" skills of high-performance teams

- Select representatives for Design Team/s

- Develop a charter for Design Team (boundaries, mission, purpose, and goals)

PHASE III:
REDESIGN

The Steering Committee selects the portion of the organization to redesign and then appoints one or more design teams to look at the entire present system and suggest ways it can be redesigned to optimize technology and people.

Members of the Design Team should be representatives of all levels and functions of the area to be redesigned. There should be experts on the area and "big picture" people who can think creatively.

> **The Design Team usually consists of:**
> - Some members of the Steering Committee
> - Key managers/supervisors/team leaders
> - Key functional people with technical expertise
> - Workers from the area to be redesigned
> - "Big Picture" creative people

Purpose of Design Team:

- Design the "best way" to produce the product or deliver the service.
- Analyze the needs of the outside customers, vendors, the government, etc. who exert an external influence on the organization. Examine how the organization is currently responding to these environmental demands.
- Examine how the present system works technically. The team studies how the entire system functions: how and where errors (variances) occur, what raw materials are needed, quality requirements, etc. They analyze the current flow of the process and determine how the technical system could be redesigned.
- Analyze how the present social system works and how redesign could create increased work satisfaction, job enrichment, job coordination, cross-functional relationships, and new roles for leaders and support people.
- Examine every aspect of the current system: hiring, firing, training, planning, scheduling, compensating, etc. and look for opportunities to improve these systems to support the new philosophy, values, and vision the new organization will embody.

- Read, attend workshops, interview customers, employees, vendors, suppliers, etc. and visit other companies.
- Make presentations to Steering and other groups on the status of their findings and receive valuable feedback and input on various work design proposals under consideration. Everyone's involvement is very important. People who actually do the work need to say how feasible the new design is. Free and open discussions are crucial to getting everyone's involvement, and ultimately, everyone's commitment to the new design.

- Prepare a design and implementation proposal. The plan is discussed with all affected parties before it is approved by the Steering Committee.
- Usually a pilot group is then chosen either by asking for a group of volunteers who want to do this or by picking a group because they meet certain criteria and would have the best chance of succeeding. Then, other teams are added gradually.
- The Design Team phase usually takes an average of 3–6 months depending on whether the members work at redesigning full or part-time.

Variations on the Design Team Model have taken the following forms:

- Several design teams meet simultaneously (each team has a different part of the business to assess (i.e., technological, social, environmental). Having several teams work simultaneously can speed-up the process and create more opportunities for involving larger numbers of people.

- The search conference model involves several conferences with large groups of people (50–100) attending. Each conference has a different theme (i.e., customer, technical, social, future vision, etc.) and lasts several days. This model also speeds-up the process (from years to months) and involves everyone in the design process because everyone can attend at least one of the conferences. It also avoids the tendency for design teams to be viewed as "elitist." By including more people the final design can be implemented with more commitment because everyone was involved in creating it. It doesn't have to be "sold" to people because everyone understands the rationale for it.

Activities of Design Team:

- Read
- Visit Sites
- Attend workshops/conferences
- Team building to become more effective in working together and to appreciate what they're asking others to do by directly experiencing how difficult it is to become a high-performing team
- Conduct in-depth environmental, technical, & social analysis of current system
- Post minutes of meetings
- Conduct presentations/walk-through sessions where they:
  —present what they're doing
  —keep everyone abreast of their activities
  —ask for input from others
  —involve others in their activities
- Make presentations to Steering Committee
- Finally, present the new design with recommendations for implementing pilot/s.
- Continue to meet for a period of time after implementation to support pilot, assess its progress, and apply what's been learned to next redesign.

Examples of *Environmental* Analysis:

- Who are our customers?
- What do they want?
- What are our current & future market demands?
- What external influences impact us (i.e., government)?
- What is our relationship with our vendors & suppliers?
- What is our competitive advantage & how do we maximize it?

Examples of *Technical* Analysis:

- Identify key criteria in evaluating the current technical system
- Chart the current work flow process/es
- Identify key variances
- Draw a layout of the system (i.e., equipment, departmental boundaries).
- Collect data
- Construct a variance matrix
- Examine where and why delays occur
- Examine where and why rework is required
- Recommend redesign that optimizes the technical system

Examples of *Social* Analysis:

- Identify the norms (unwritten rules) that govern how people and groups behave in the workplace
- Examine relationships between workers, supervisors, managers, union, men, women, races, etc.
- Examine morale, spirit, enthusiasm, motivation, etc.
- What stories have become legends and what values, philosophy, work ethic do these convey to people?
- How are new employees treated? . . . trained? . . . initiated?
- How is performance measured?
- How is performance rewarded?
- What is the current skill level of people?
- How are people assessed?
- How are people promoted?
- What training have people received?
- What is the current level of employee involvement?
- Finally, recommend a redesign that optimizes the social system

IMPORTANT REDESIGN CONSIDERATIONS:

- Each organization has to create an original design that uniquely fits their workplace. It has to make sense to everyone and take into account what is best for the process and the people.

- This socio-tech process of designing better work for everyone has worked in new sites and redesigns of traditional factories and offices (with union and non-union work forces).

- Fragmented jobs are turned into whole tasks that a team completes for its customers.

- The aim is for everyone to understand how the whole system works and to be empowered to act on behalf of a customer.

- Action-orientation is the goal. High-quality decisions can be made swiftly by teams of highly committed workers who are empowered to do what is right.

- Designs should include a responsibility chart which shows how the team will, over time, take over the tasks performed by staff and supervision. This transition plan helps everyone receive training and gradually adjust to new roles. in the organization.

- Establishing this new way of working usually takes years to produce gains in productivity and quality. (Although some positive results, such as, employee morale, attitude, and commitment will become evident as soon as trust improves.)

- Everyone's job will change (from CEO to frontline person). This is a very exciting and frustrating time. Not everyone can work in this new environment and options should be made available to everyone.

- As the organization flattens and people are trained, there will be less need for traditional supervision and management. Part of redesign will be to rethink the role of leadership. High-performance organizations need leaders (on teams for coordinating and outside teams for managing the boundaries). As teams transition to high-performance, displaced supervisors and managers should be given choices on their new roles (training, facilitation, team coordination, technical expert to several teams, etc.) They also need training to prepare them for their present and future roles.

PHASE IV:
IMPLEMENTATION

- The Design Team with the Steering Committee's approval selects the first pilot or pilots
    - —usually selected because the area seems likely to be successful
    - —sometimes chosen because a new product or process provides a unique opportunity to start fresh with a new area and people who have volunteered to be part of the pilot

Purpose of Phase IV:

- To implement this new way of working that embodies the new values, mission, and culture
- To learn how to make the pilot succeed and apply this learning to subsequent pilots

Activities During Phase IV:

- Team Building for the pilot/s so they will become a "real" team and be more effective/productive
- Training for Team Members (does not occur all at once, but is "just-in-time")
    - —technical training (including cross-training)
    - —administrative training (what traditional supervision used to do)
    - —high-performance training (communication, effective meetings, new roles & responsibilities, conflict management, decision-making, problem-solving, etc.)
- Training for Team Leaders/Facilitators/Managers
- Measures that enable team to see how it's doing in terms of quality, customer service, quantity, team effectiveness, etc. Based on these measures, the team is able to self-correct and implement improvements.

PHASE V:
ASSESSMENT,
EXPANSION, &
CONTINUOUS LEARNING

- Design Team stays intact for a period of time to provide support for the pilot/s and to learn what's needed for subsequent teams during expansion.

- Steering Committee also continues to meet and lead the change effort.

- Original design is modified to accommodate the realities of the work and the people on the team

- Measurement & assessment of pilot/s provides information on what revisions need to be made before expanding to other teams

- Pilot/s given business information, knowledge & skills, and decision-making power

- Design Team & Steering Committee analyze present systems and structures and how they support the new design or act as barriers:
  —organization structure
  —appraisal system
  —reward system
  —job classifications
  —hiring/firing
  —career development
  —etc.

- Pilot provides valuable learning on how the new system performs and what it needs in order to succeed

- Based on this new learning, the Steering Committee decides how to proceed:
  —Redesign another area, expand to more teams, etc.
  —Decide how to build learning and continual redesign and renewal into the system by:
    - determining what training should be on-going
    - determining how to apply continuous learning throughout the system
    - anticipating change
    - involving everyone in the continual renewal of the organization

NOTES:

ACTION FIVE

Involving All Key Stakeholders

- *Ten Common Mistakes Made During Change Efforts & How to Prevent/Repair Them*

- *High-Involvement Exercises:*
  - *Organizational Climate Assessment-"How Conducive Is Your Current Organization Climate to 'Real' Empowerment?"*
  - *"Critical Questions" for Planning Change*
  - *Consensus Building Exercise:*
    The "Essential Ingredients" of High-Performance
    - *Debriefing/Discussion Guide*

In order to achieve the kinds of changes we're talking about—empowerment, involvement, high-performance/self-direction—all stakeholders must be involved in the process, and ideally, at the very outset. Any group that is left out will resist, causing major disruption.

Many of the problems that beset change efforts and, ultimately, bring about their downfall have to do with lack of involvement. The following list explores some of the common mistakes we've encountered and examines possible solutions:

TEN COMMON MISTAKES MADE DURING CHANGE IMPLEMENTATION & HOW TO AVOID OR REPAIR THEM

Mistake #1
Top Leadership Doesn't Get Directly Involved

Solution: Do everything possible to invite top leadership's participation. Supply them with books and articles, invite them to conferences/training sessions, visit sites together, etc.

- Make a compelling case for why they should be on the Steering Committee/Quality Council because nothing is more important than leading the organization into the future. Only by directly participating will they change their own values, attitudes, and behaviors. If this is delegated, top leadership will never understand or appreciate the very ideas they say they favor and they will become a barrier to the very things they say they want.

Mistake #2
Management Changes During the Transition & Original Sponsor Leaves

Solution: Since new management may or may not want to continue the changes begun by their predecessor, provide for this in advance by building-in a succession plan. The best ones provide for interviewing and selecting the new leader based on his/her knowledge of and support for high-performance.

Mistake #3
Steering Committee Composed of Management Only

Solution: If you've already started but omitted representatives of key stakeholders, invite them to join now. The consequences of having a management *only* committee are:

- By leaving out key stakeholders (union, workers, supervisors, middle managers, etc.) you guarantee their resistance.
- There won't be enough divergence of opinion or creative tension because fear will cause people to agree too quickly.
- Viewpoints & valuable information that can only come directly from people will be omitted.
- It sends out wrong symbolic message that this is going to be business as usual with management calling all the shots.

Mistake #4
People Who Feel Left Out Resist

Solution: Find a way to involve everyone (search conferences, task forces, committees, study groups, open forums, meetings, etc.) Involvement builds commitment and everyone's input will make the final outcome better. People don't resist change when they've participated in creating it.

Mistake #5
Lack of Buy-In From Managers & Supervisors

Solution: Involve leaders in redesigning their own roles. Give them choices about what they'll be doing as the organization flattens and there is gradually less need for as many managers and supervisors. Finally, provide training in the new skills they'll need for their new roles (coaching, facilitation, coordination, boundary management, training/teaching, technical advising, etc.)

Mistake #6
Failure To Involve the Union As Full Partner

Solution: Where high-performance has succeeded in union environments, the union was involved at the very beginning and treated as a full-partner in joint decision-making concerning everything about the change effort. When this is done, the union is a powerful advocate, but when left out, it's a powerful adversary. Union leadership should be part of the education and search process at the very outset. When joint partnership is achieved, and years of mistrust and adversarial roles are overcome, high-performing teams can be very successful in union environments. Examples of this are NUMMI, Saturn, Xerox, Procter & Gamble, GE, Westinghouse, IBM, Polaroid, Rohm & Haas, and many others.

High-performance systems give unions things they've always wanted:

- joint decision-making power on important leadership committees (including boards of directors)
- job security by being world-class competitive
- greater worker satisfaction
- better reward systems
- work security assurance in exchange for flexible job classifications and less restrictive work rules
- better work climate where trust replaces time clocks, workers are treated with respect, and everyone is an "owner"
- significant decision-making power

Mistake #7
Final Design Not Radical Enough

Solution: Give the Design Team a blank slate (i.e., *"What would you do if there were no constraints?"*) With too many constraints, the final design may lack the creativity needed for breakthrough improvements.

Make sure the Steering Committee really becomes a team and establishes consensus on core values, vision, and mission.

Unless underlying attitudes, values, and assumptions change; the traditional culture will still be the same.

Provide team development for Steering and Design so that open, honest communication occurs and everyone isn't just agreeing with "the boss." (An outside consultant can be helpful in keeping the group honest.)

Make sure the scope of the redesign is broad enough to cut across existing boundaries of functions and departments and focuses on an entire core process.

Mistake #8
A "Quick-Fix" Mentality

Solution: Create a long-range plan (5 or 10 years) to show you're in this for the long haul. Set realistic expectations so people will know what to expect. Demonstrate faith that this will work over time by committing resources and assuring everyone that they will succeed.

Mistake #9
Not Enough Training

Solution: Commit to training everyone in the organization (not all at once but over a period of time). Establish learning at the heart of the organization and commit to training forever.

Mistake #10
Creating Teams In Name Only

Solution: Make sure the work is analyzed and redesigned/reengineered first, before designating teams. Then, train people to become a high-performing team (technical skills training, administrative skills training, and interpersonal skills training).

Continue team growth and development by providing:

- information
- training
- decision-making power
- rewards tied to performance

The following HIGH-INVOLVEMENT EXERCISES are vehicles for involving everyone in the change process. They can be used by:

- Steering Committees
- Design Teams
- Task Forces
- Study Groups
- Committees
- Work Teams

Their purpose is to help you:

- Involve
- Educate
- Examine Assumptions
- Discuss
- Reach Consensus on Major Issues Concerning Empowerment, Employee Involvement, & High-Performance

HIGH-INVOLVEMENT EXERCISE:

Organizational Climate Assessment

Learning Objective:

To help individuals and teams assess and reach consensus on the current organizational climate and how conducive it is to achieving empowerment.

Directions:

Step One- Individual Exercise

Circle the number that best describes your organization as it is now. (10 min.)

1. SHARED VISION, MISSION, VALUES?

1	2	3	4	5
THERE IS NO SHARED VISION, MISSION, VALUES	STATED BUT NOT KNOWN BY EVERYONE	KNOWN BUT NOT LIVED	HAS MEANING TO MOST PEOPLE	EVERYONE KNOWS AND LIVES BY THEM

2. PARTICIPATIVE LEADERSHIP?

1	2	3	4	5
AUTOCRATIC LEADERSHIP	VERY TRADITIONAL	LEADERS TRYING TO CHANGE	LEADERS' ROLE REDEFINED & BEHAVIOR CHANGING	NO TRADITIONAL BOSSES; LEADERS ARE COACHES, RESOURCES, ETC.

3. A CLIMATE OF TRUST?

1	2	3	4	5
NO TRUST	VERY LITTLE TRUST	TRUST IS BETTER THAN IT USED TO BE	TRUST EXISTS BETWEEN MOST PEOPLE & GROUPS BUT NOT EVERYONE	VERY TRUSTING CLIMATE

4. COMMUNICATION?

1	2	3	4	5
POOR COMMUNICATION	SOME COMMUNICATION BUT NOT ENOUGH	COMMUNICATION GETTING BETTER	QUALITY & QUANTITY OF COMMUNICATION GOOD	EXCELLENT COMMUNICATION

5. INVOLVEMENT?

1	2	3	4	5
MANAGEMENT ONLY INVOLVED IN CHANGE EFFORT	KEY PEOPLE & GROUPS NOT INVOLVED YET	OPPORTUNITIES EXIST FOR EVERYONE TO GET INVOLVED	MOST PEOPLE INVOLVED	EVERYONE INVOLVED

6. INFORMATION?

1	2	3	4	5
PEOPLE DO NOT GET INFORMATION THEY NEED TO DO QUALITY WORK	ONLY GET INFORMATION LEADERS WANT THEM TO HAVE	GET SOME NEEDED INFORMATION	GET MOST NEEDED INFORMATION	GET ALL RELEVANT BUSINESS INFORMATION

7. HIGH-PERFORMANCE TEAMS?

1	2	3	4	5
NOT ORGANIZED INTO TEAMS	HAVE TEMPORARY GROUPS BUT NOT REALLY TEAMS	HAVE SOME WORK TEAMS	HAVE WORK TEAMS AND WORKING ON MAKING THEM MORE EFFECTIVE	HAVE HIGH-PERFORMING TEAMS THROUGHOUT THE ORGANIZATION

8. TRAINING?

1	2	3	4	5
PEOPLE HAVE RECEIVED LITTLE OR NO TRAINING	SOME PEOPLE HAVE RECEIVED TRAINING	MOST PEOPLE HAVE RECEIVED SOME TRAINING	EVERYONE HAS RECEIVED SOME TRAINING	EVERYONE IS CONSTANTLY TRAINED AND WILL BE FOREVER

9. DECISION-MAKING?

1	2	3	4	5
ALL DECISIONS ARE MADE BY LEADERSHIP	MOST DECISIONS MADE BY LEADERS	WORKERS MAKING SOME KEY DECISIONS	EVERYONE MAKING SOME KEY DECISIONS	MAJORITY OF DECISIONS MADE BY CONSENSUS

10. MEASUREMENT?

1	2	3	4	5
PERFORMANCE IS NOT MEASURED	PERFORMANCE MONITORED BY SUPERVISION	OUTPUT ONLY MEASURED	OUTPUT, QUALITY, AND CUSTOMER SERVICE MEASURED	PEOPLE & TEAMS MEASURE HOW THEY'RE DOING AND WAYS TO IMPROVE

11. ORGANIZATIONAL SYSTEMS & STRUCTURES?

1	2	3	4	5
SYSTEMS NOT COMPATIBLE WITH EMPOWERMENT	JUST BEGINNING TO EXAMINE SYSTEMS & STRUCTURES	REDESIGN TEAM WORKING ON SYSTEMS & STRUCTURES	MOST SYSTEMS & STRUCTURES HAVE BEEN REENGINEERED/ REDESIGNED	ALL SYSTEMS & STRUCTURES HAVE BEEN REDESIGNED/ REGINEERED TO SUPPORT TEAMS

12. REWARDS?

1	2	3	4	5
REWARDS NOT TIED TO PERFORMANCE	JUST BEGINNING TO EXAMINE THIS	TASK FORCE WORKING ON THIS	EXPERIMENTING WITH NEW REWARD SYSTEMS	REWARDS TIED TO PERFORMANCE

Step Two- Team Exercise

After everyone has completed circling their choices for all twelve questions, write your individual answers in the column below marked, "Individual Score." Discuss your individual scores and reach consensus* as a team on each of the twelve questions. Write these answers in the column marked, "Team Score." (35 min.)

*See "Guidelines for Reaching Consensus" on page 7.

Question:	Individual Score:	Team Score:	Actions:
#1			
#2			
#3			
#4			
#5			
#6			
#7			
#8			
#9			
#10			
#11			
#12			

Step Three- Team Exercise

After reaching consensus on each of the twelve questions, discuss and agree on actions that need to be taken to increase your "current" score. Write these in the "Actions" column. (15 min.)

"CRITICAL QUESTIONS"

For Planning Change Efforts

Learning Objective:

To help individuals and teams think through, discuss, and agree on critical issues in planning change efforts.

Directions:

Step One- Individual Exercise

Read and answer the following questions: (15 min.)

1. As you examine your current organization, is there a problem or exploitable opportunity? (Examples would be: improved customer service, high quality, lower costs, shorter cycle times, etc.)

_____

_____

_____

_____

_____

_____

2. Does the problem or opportunity involve employee motivation, work satisfaction, or work effectiveness?

_____

_____

_____

_____

_____

_____

3. Might the present design of work be partially responsible for the problem/s?

_____

_____

_____

_____

_____

_____

4. And if so, what aspects of the job/s most need improvements?

_____

_____

_____

_____

_____

5. How ready is the work force for change?

_____

_____

_____

_____

_____

_____

6. How compatible is the present leadership style with employee involvement? (Are leaders participative? Do they share information and decision-making power with their people?)

_____

_____

_____

_____

_____

_____

_____

7. How compatible is the present company culture with employee involvement?

_____

_____

_____

_____

_____

_____

8. Does your organization presently have some form of employee involvement (i.e., Quality Circles, Problem-solving Teams, Process Improvement Teams)?

_____

_____

_____

_____

_____

_____

9. Is your market healthy enough to assure people they will not lose their jobs as a result of productivity improvements?

_____

_____

_____

_____

_____

_____

_____

10. Does top management understand what its new role would be?

_____

_____

_____

_____

_____

11. Are managers and supervisors in favor of this change?

_____

_____

_____

_____

_____

_____

12. Is this change viewed as a long-term commitment (2–4 years at the least)?

_____

_____

_____

_____

_____

_____

13. Is the organization willing to commit the necessary resources (time and money)?

_____

_____

_____

14. How will organizational systems have to change (i.e., appraisal systems, organization structure, reward systems)?

_____

_____

_____

15. Is this change seen as a participatory process involving everyone, and not a "Program-of-the-Month" imposed on people?

_____

_____

_____

_____

After answering the first fifteen questions, summarize your thoughts with these last questions:

16. What do you see as the drawbacks involved in changing?
    Check (✔) what you believe are potential drawbacks.

☐ Time off the job
☐ Time for training
☐ Time for meetings
☐ Money for training

☐ Possible productivity dip while people learn new roles
☐ Productivity gains only after 1 or 2 years
☐ Too much change

Resistance from:
☐ Workers
☐ Supervisors
☐ Managers
☐ Support Functions
☐ Union

Other drawbacks:

_____

_____

17. What do you see as the benefits?
    Check (✔) what you believe are potential benefits.

☐ Better customer service
☐ Higher quality
☐ Productivity gains
☐ Faster response time
☐ Lower costs
☐ Motivated employees
☐ Innovation
☐ Improved job satisfaction/morale
☐ Higher commitment & sense of ownership
☐ Less supervision needed
☐ Fewer people needed to do better quality work at lower costs

☐ More flexibility from multi-skilled work team members
☐ Constant improvement of everything by everybody
☐ More employee involvement, therefore, more information, responsibility, accountability, and decision-making shared by everyone

☐ Improved performance
☐ Attraction & retention of employees
☐ Better work methods to increase rate of output
☐ Reduced need for support people
☐ Development of technical skills
☐ Increased problem-solving ability

Other benefits:

_____

_____

_____

18. At this time *my* recommendation is:

_____

_____

_____

_____

Step Two- Team Exercise

After everyone has finished completing the questions, discuss and reach consensus* on each question. (40 min.)

*See *"Guidelines for Reaching Consensus"* on page 7.

Step Three- Team Exercise

Reach consensus on what the next step should be. (10 min.)

_____

_____

_____

_____

_____

_____

_____

_____

HIGH-INVOLVEMENT EXERCISE:

The "Essential Ingredients" of High-Performance

Learning Objective:

To think through and reach consensus on some key issues involving high-performance.

Directions:

Step One- Individual Exercise

After reading each of the 25 statements, place an "A" next to the ones you AGREE with; a "D" next to the ones you DISAGREE with. (10 min.)

( ) 1.   Changing a traditional organization into a high-performing one demands a compelling business reason.

( ) 2.   The best reason to change is survival, even if people feel the situation is hopeless.

( ) 3.   Support from top management is not that important if you have several very committed work groups of frontline employees who want to become high-performing work teams.

( ) 4.   Top management must get personally involved and serve on the Steering Committee if the change effort is to succeed.

( ) 5.   Trust is desirable in moving to high-performance, but not essential.

( ) 6.   To build trust in an organization, the Steering Committee of top and middle management must spend about one year working together on the concept prior to discussing it with the rest of the organization.

( ) 7.   Involving all the stakeholders in the organization is not important if top and middle management is committed to the change effort.

( ) 8.   Unions have nothing to gain from changing to high-performance.

( ) 9.   Involving everyone is the only way to gain the kind of commitment to change high-performance requires.

( )10.   Managers and supervisors' buy-in is critical, but not essential.

( )11.   Alternate career paths need to be created for displaced supervisors and managers.

(*continued*)

( )12.   Everyone needs to be involved and serve on committees, task forces, and teams.

( )13.   Communication and sharing new information is the most important first step.

( )14.   High-performance is best undertaken when companies are growing, not downsizing.

( )15.   Work security assurance is an essential ingredient because it frees people to work on productivity improvements and not worry about working themselves out of a job.

( )16.   The first training that workers and leaders need is in the new skills and concepts required for high-performance.

( )17.   Time and money for training is the number one barrier to successful implementation of high-performance.

( )18.   Employees should be given information on *all* aspects of the business.

( )19.   We cannot ask people to be responsible, if we don't give them the pertinent information they need.

( )20.   Decision-making power should only be turned over to people after they've been given information and training.

( )21.   Empowerment means being furnished information, given the training to use it, and the authority to make decisions.

( )22.   High-performing teams collect data on how they're doing so management can accurately assess and discipline them.

( )23.   Only mature teams (Stage 4—two or more years) should be able to hire and fire.

( )24.   Reward systems do not need to change because money is not a motivator.

( )25.   In order for high-performance to be achieved, all systems (measurement, appraisal, reward, and promotion) need to be changed.

Step Two- Team Exercise

When everyone has finished, discuss your individual answers and reach consensus* on whether you agree or disagree with each statement. (You can all agree, disagree, or change the wording of the statements in order to reach consensus. (45 min.)

*See "*Guidelines for Reaching Consensus*" on page 7.

DISCUSSION GUIDE:

Debriefing The "Essential Ingredients" of High-Performance

The purpose of this exercise really isn't to provide "right" and "wrong" answers to the 25 questions, but rather to help the members of an organization engage in discussion and reach consensus on the following key issues:

- How important is a "business reason" in driving change? What are your compelling business reasons?
- Is survival the best reason? If people feel the situation is hopeless, what should be done?
- Do you have support from top management? If you don't, what can you do to obtain it? If you don't get support from top management, what is likely to happen?
- How much trust is in your organization now? How essential is trust? What historically caused the lack of trust? What can be done to increase it?
- Should *everything* about the Steering Committee be communicated to the rest of the organization? What would be the consequences of secrecy?
- Are all the key stakeholders represented on the Steering Committee? Are groups left out? Is the committee diverse in its make-up? Should anyone else be included at this point?
- Has the union been included as a full-partner?
- How committed are the people of the organization, at this point, to making the changes succeed?

- Have managers and supervisors been involved? Have they bought-in? How have they been affected so far? How are they likely to be affected? Have their roles been redesigned? Have they received training? Have they been given work security assurance? Have they been given choices about their new roles?
- How effective has two-way communication been thus far? Are there any rumors? Do a majority of people feel informed?
- Is the company growing or downsizing? What effect has this had?
- Has there been work security assurance? What has been the result?
- Has training been provided?
- Has business information been given to everyone?
- Has significant decision-making power been pushed down the organization so that everyone is making the decisions they should be making? If not, why not?
- Is there agreement on what empowerment means in this organization? Is it happening? Why or why not?
- Is there agreement on what high-performance means?
- Who should measure the progress of teams: The teams themselves or management? Which style is more in accordance with the values, mission, vision of the new organization?
- How should appraisal be handled? Who knows best what work is ac-

complished: team members themselves or leaders outside the team?

- How should discipline be handled?
- What should teams be doing in the early stages (first year) compared with later stages? Is there a transition plan to let teams know what's expected of them? Do leaders and support people know what their role will be?
- What is the present system of compensation? Is it based on performance? Does the present system help or hurt team culture? How could rewards be tied to performance?
- Do appraisal, reward, promotion, and measurement need review to see how effective they are in promoting high-performance, empowerment, and employee involvement?

NOTES:

NOTES:

ACTION SIX

Sharing Decision-making Power

- *Choosing the Best Decision-making Style*
- *Delegating Not "Dumping"*
- *Decision-making & Empowerment*
- *Criteria for a "Good" Decision*
- *What Kinds of Decisions Can High-Performing Teams Make?*
- *Empowering Teams*
- *High-Involvement Exercise: Creating a Transition Plan*
  - *Sample Transition Plan*
  - *High-Involvement Team Exercise*

CHOOSING THE *BEST* DECISION-MAKING STYLE

To understand why high-performing teams have an advantage in the area of decision-making, let's look at 3 styles of decision-making and the pluses and minuses of each style:

> ## STYLE #1: DIRECTIVE
> One person with authority makes the decision for everyone.

This has been the prevailing style in traditional organizations. The boss makes the decisions for everyone. The chief advantage is speed and in a crisis or emergency this may be the best style. When speed is called for to avert a disaster, one person with authority has to make a decision quickly.

But the disadvantages of this style are so numerous that we are seeing it used less-and-less. Here are just some of the disadvantages:

- Only one person's wisdom, facts, knowledge, expertise, etc. is being used. (The people who may know the most are not being consulted.)

- Others may not agree with the decision and will not carry it out.
- People will feel left out of the decision-making process and may not feel committed to the decision or responsible for making it succeed.
- There is no opportunity for group synergy.
- The *how* and *why* of the decision may not be readily apparent.

> ## STYLE #2: CONSULTATIVE
> One person with authority makes the decision after consulting with everyone.

Style #2 is slower than Style #1, but taps more knowledge, wisdom, and ideas from other people. This increases the likelihood of a higher quality decision in the end. Commitment to carry out the decision also increases since now people are asked for input and feel more involved. Nevertheless, only one person with authority will make the final decision. Many leaders believe this style is participative, but it is only so in a very limited way.

> ## STYLE #3: PARTICIPATIVE
> **The whole team decides together how to solve a problem, schedule work, plan & prioritize, set goals & objectives, make buying decisions, etc.**

This style is most prevalent in high-performing teams where underlying assumptions are that:

- Everyone has some valuable knowledge to contribute, so putting "our heads together" will produce higher quality results.
- The commitment of the people involved is essential for making the decision succeed.
- The team together can be more creative—synergistic than people working alone.
- Decision-making is an opportunity to build the team.
- Empowerment means being able to make decisions.
- The people doing the work are the best experts on the work.
- The team, by concentrating on planning, scheduling, performing, checking and improving the work, frees leaders to do more cross-functional work, provide resources, coach, and focus on long term planning. Turning decision-making over to the team enables leaders to do the real job of leadership and let team members manage the work.

DELEGATING *NOT* DUMPING:

Participative decision-making has great potential provided the team is properly prepared in the following ways:

- The team is given the necessary information
- The team is given the proper training in decision-making, problem-solving, interpersonal skills (communication, listening, etc.).

There is risk involved in this style. The team may not make the best decision (especially a new team or one that has not been accustomed to making decisions together). The worst thing a leader can do is reverse a decision once he/she has handed it over because this will hurt his/her credibility. So, a wise leader makes the first decision-making activities as risk-free as possible by handing over easy decisions first.

It helps to remember that the job of leadership is to set direction by stating goals or tasks and then a wise leader gives the team the autonomy to perform the task as they see fit. As long as the team members believe they have chosen the best way, it may be the best way for them, even though it is not how the leader would do it.

What Kinds of Decisions Can High-Performing Teams Make?

After they receive the proper information and training, high-performing teams can make decisions on:

- ☐ Setting goals
- ☐ Vacation scheduling
- ☐ Deciding who does what each day
- ☐ Solving problems of all types
- ☐ Making improvements on: How the work is done, the quality of the product, the customer service
- ☐ Safety
- ☐ Housekeeping
- ☐ Making minor repairs and performing routine maintenance
- ☐ Stopping the work in order to address quality problems

- ☐ Working with customers (internal & external), suppliers, vendors
- ☐ Assessing peers
- ☐ Hiring & firing work team members
- ☐ Managing budgets
- ☐ Assessing & addressing training needs
- ☐ Measuring performance of individuals and the team
- ☐ Making compensation decisions
- ☐ Deciding which team member gets a limited resource

Place a check ☑ in the boxes indicating decisions your team currently makes.

Criteria For A "Good" Decision:

A good decision has two components: Quality and Commitment. A *Quality* decision takes into account the relevant facts and makes good use of those facts. It is a logical decision with sound reasoning behind it.

The second element of a good decision is that in addition to having quality, it also has the *Commitment* of the people who will carry it out.

A decision that has quality, but does not have the commitment of people, is useless because no one will carry it out and make it succeed. On the other hand, a poor quality decision that everyone acts on is equally wasteful and destructive.

Both Quality and Commitment are critical to effective decision-making. It is in this area that teams have their greatest advantage. When teams are provided with the right information, training, and the power to make decisions, they can produce high-quality and high-commitment decisions.

Decision-Making & Empowerment

How decisions are made is critical to organizations since real power is the ability to make decisions. All three styles of decision-making are needed in organizations, but we have traditionally over used Style #1-Directive and underused Style #3-Participative. Empowerment succeeds when decisions are made at all levels of the organization and the people who know the work best are given the power to put their knowledge, skills, talents, ideas, and suggestions into practice.

EMPOWERING TEAMS

High-performing teams are empowered by increasing their information, training, skills, and decision-making authority.

Several factors need to be taken into consideration when determining WHAT decisions to turn over and WHEN:

- the nature of the work
- the culture of the organization
- contract agreements with unions
- skill level of team members (*readiness*)
- attitudes of team members towards taking on more responsibility and authority (*willingness*)
- vision of future organization (i.e., Are self-directed teams with no traditional supervision the ultimate aim?)

The key is to do what makes sense in terms of the nature of the work and the work force. Both of these factors are unique to a given organization, but as a general rule it is best to begin with easier tasks, such as, vacation scheduling and proceed to more difficult decisions only after people have the necessary information and training. Eventually, teams will need technical, administrative, and interpersonal training.

Some teams will never hire and fire. Some teams will only do this after they've been operating for two or more years. A transition plan is very important because it let's the team members know they're not expected to do everything all at once. They'll be given information, training, resources, and support as they gradually take on more and more responsibilities. A transition plan also lets everyone know the extent of empowerment that will eventually be achieved (i.e., Are the teams going to hire and fire?).

There is no limit to what a high-performing team can do. Teams keep growing and developing as they're given more information, knowledge, skills, and decision-making power.

HIGH-INVOLVEMENT EXERCISE:

Creating a Transition Plan

Learning Objective:

To create a transition plan for "handing-off" tasks/responsibilities to a team in stages so they have time to prepare and receive the proper training. Also, to delineate frontline leader's role and responsibilities at each stage.

Directions:

Step One- Individual Task

Read through the list of 53 tasks/responsibilities" on the the next two pages. All of these 53 items could be done by a mature (Stage IV) team.

After selecting a particular team at your site, choose the tasks/responsibilities you think a Stage I (first six months) team could do. Place a "1" in the Stage I column next to the items you've chosen. Then, place a "2" to indicate the items a team could do at Stage II (next six months). Do the same for Stage III (after one year) and Stage IV (after two or more years). If an item does not pertain, leave it blank. If there are items you'd like to add, you can write these in the blanks provided. (15 min.)

Step Two- Team Task

After everyone has finished making their selections, discuss them as a team and reach consensus* on a transition plan. Write this plan on the page entitled: "Team's Transition Plan." (30 min.)

*See *"Guidelines for Reaching Consensus"* on page 7.

"Individual" TRANSITION PLAN

Tasks/Responsibilities:	Stage I	Stage II	Stage III	Stage IV
1. Decide on Goals for Team				
2. Cross-train Team Members				
3. Hire New Team Members				
4. Do Peer Appraisals				
5. Represent Organization at Outside Meetings				
6. Decide Resource Needs for Team				
7. Recognize Team Members for Superior Work				
8. Schedule Vacations				
9. Select Team Leader				
10. Meet with Other Teams/Shifts				
11. Decide Job Assignments within Team				
12. Decide/Implement Process Improvements				
13. Determine Training Needs				
14. Make Cost Improvements				
15. Make Quality Improvements				
16. Measure Team's Performance				
17. Schedule Work of Team				
18. Give Input on Engineering Changes				
19. Schedule Training				
20. Schedule Overtime				
21. Work with Internal Customers				
22. Work with Vendors/Suppliers				
23. Coordinate Between Shifts/Teams				
24. Maintain Safety & Housekeeping				
25. Keep Abreast of Goals & Objectives of Top Mgmt.				
26. Work with External Customers				
27. Monitor Individual Skill Development of Team Members				
28. Secure Resources for Team				
29. Resolve Conflicts Among Team Members				
30. Prepare Reports on Team's Progress on Goals				

"Individual" TRANSITION PLAN

Tasks/Responsibilities:	Stage I	Stage II	Stage III	Stage IV
31. Facilitate Team Meetings				
32. Monitor Progress of Multiple Teams				
33. Motivate Team Members				
34. Prepare Budgets				
35. Resolve Personnel Issues on Team				
36. Inform Team of Needs of Other Teams				
37. Define Areas of Team's Responsibility				
38. Align Team Goals with Individual Career Goals				
39. Distribute Resources				
40. Coach & Counsel Team Members				
41. Identify New Business Opportunities				
42. Inform Mgmt. of Status of Team's Work				
43. Fire Team Members				
44. Develop Standards				
45. New Product Development				
46. Represent Team on Committees				
47. Develop Criteria to Assess Team's Performance				
48. Set Cost Reduction Targets				
49. Develop Compensation Systems				
50. Have Input on Hiring & Firing				
51. Monitor Continuous Improvement				
52. Continual Renewal/Redesign of Systems				
53. Do Long-Range Planning				

"Team" TRANSITION PLAN

Tasks/Responsibilities:	Stage I	Stage II	Stage III	Stage IV
1. Decide on Goals for Team				
2. Cross-train Team Members				
3. Hire New Team Members				
4. Do Peer Appraisals				
5. Represent Organization at Outside Meetings				
6. Decide Resource Needs for Team				
7. Recognize Team Members for Superior Work				
8. Schedule Vacations				
9. Select Team Leader (within team)				
10. Meet with Other Teams/Shifts				
11. Decide Job Assignments within Team				
12. Decide/Implement Process Improvements				
13. Determine Training Needs				
14. Make Cost Improvements				
15. Make Quality Improvements				
16. Measure Team's Performance				
17. Schedule Work of Team				
18. Give Input on Engineering Changes				
19. Schedule Training				
20. Schedule Overtime				
21. Work with Internal Customers				
22. Work with Vendors/Suppliers				
23. Coordinate Between Shifts/Teams				
24. Maintain Safety & Housekeeping				
25. Keep Abreast of Goals & Objectives of Top Mgmt.				
26. Work with Extornal Customors				
27. Monitor Individual Skill Development of Team Members				
28. Secure Resources for Team				
29. Resolve Conflicts Among Team Members				
30. Prepare Reports on Team's Progress on Goals				

"Team" TRANSITION PLAN

Tasks/Responsibilities:	Stage I	Stage II	Stage III	Stage IV
31. Facilitate Team Meetings				
32. Monitor Progress of Multiple Teams				
33. Motivate Team Members				
34. Prepare Budgets				
35. Resolve Personnel Issues on Team				
36. Inform Team of Needs of Other Teams				
37. Define Areas of Team's Responsibility				
38. Align Team Goals with Individual Career Goals				
39. Distribute Resources				
40. Coach & Counsel Team Members				
41. Identify New Business Opportunities				
42. Inform Mgmt. of Status of Team's Work				
43. Fire Team Members				
44. Develop Standards				
45. New Product Development				
46. Represent Team on Committees				
47. Develop Criteria to Assess Team's Performance				
48. Set Cost Reduction Targets				
49. Develop Compensation Systems				
50. Have Input on Hiring & Firing				
51. Monitor Continuous Improvement				
52. Continual Renewal/Redesign of Systems				
53. Do Long-Range Planning				

Step Three- Team Exercise

Write the tasks/responsibilities the team selected for each stage in the first column (Tasks/Responsibilities of Team). Then, as a team discuss and reach consensus* on the frontline leader's role at each stage.
*See *"Guidelines for Reaching Consensus"* page 7.

STAGE I

Tasks/Responsibilities of Team:	Leader's Role & Responsibilities:	Team Training Needed:

STAGE II

Tasks/Responsibilities of Team:	Leader's Role & Responsibilities:	Team Training Needed:

Step Four- Team Exercise

Discuss and reach consensus on the training needed at each stage.

STAGE III

Tasks/Responsibilities of Team:	Leader's Role & Responsibilities:	Team Training Needed:

STAGE IV

Tasks/Responsibilities of Team:	Leader's Role & Responsibilities:	Team Training Needed:

We are often asked by people who've just completed the "Transition Plan" exercise, "Is there a correct answer? A perfect transition plan?"

There really isn't because the best transition plan for your organization will have to be determined by your people and they *must* be involved in the planning and the implementation of what is decided. Your people are the experts on your organization culture, the readiness of the workers, and the work itself. Their involvement will bring expertise and commitment to the final plan.

The following pages provide a "Sample Transition Plan" to give an idea of how one might look. However, avoid the trap of adopting anyone else's plan because it may not be right for your organization and your teams. And even if it were, it would lack the involvement of your people. We advise not dictating a plan, but developing one together. Not all teams adopt exactly the same plan. There should be room for differences, as long as there are supportable reasons.

"*SAMPLE*" TRANSITION PLAN

Tasks/Responsibilities:	Stage I	Stage II	Stage III	Stage IV
1. Decide on Goals for Team	1			→
2. Cross-Train Team Members	1			→
3. Hire New Team Members			3	→
4. Do Peer Appraisals			3	→
5. Represent Organization at Outside Meetings			3	→
6. Decide Resource Needs for Team		2		→
7. Recognize Team Members for Superior Work		2		→
8. Schedule Vacations	1			→
9. Select Team Leader (within team)	1			→
10. Meet with Other Teams/Shifts		2		→
11. Decide Job Assignments within Team	1			→
12. Decide/Implement Process Improvements		2		→
13. Determine Training Needs		2		→
14. Make Cost Improvements	1			→
15. Make Quality Improvements	1			→
16. Measure Team's Performance	1			→
17. Schedule Work of Team	1			→
18. Give Input on Engineering Changes		2		→
19. Schedule Training		2		→
20. Schedule Overtime		2		→
21. Work with Internal Customers	1			→
22. Work with Vendors/Suppliers		2		→
23. Coordinate Between Shifts/Teams				4
24. Maintain Safety & Housekeeping	1			→
25. Keep Abreast of Goals & Objectives of Top Mgmt.		2		→
26. Work with External Customers		2		→
27. Monitor Individual Skill Development of Team Members			3	→
28. Secure Resources for Team			3	→
29. Resolve Conflicts Among Team Members			3	→

➤ Arrows indicate on-going tasks/responsibilities

"*SAMPLE*" TRANSITION PLAN

Tasks/Responsibilities:	Stage I	Stage II	Stage III	Stage IV
30. Prepare Reports on Team's Progress on Goals			3 ⇒	
31. Facilitate Team Meetings			3 ⇒	
32. Monitor Progress of Multiple Teams				4
33. Motivate Team Members	1 ⇒			
34. Prepare Budgets				4
35. Resolve Personnel Issues on Team			3 ⇒	
36. Inform Team of Needs of Other Teams			3 ⇒	
37. Define Areas of Team's Responsibility	1 ⇒			
38. Align Team Goals with Individual Career Goals			3 ⇒	
39. Distribute Resources			3 ⇒	
40. Coach & Counsel Team Members		2 ⇒		
41. Identify New Business Opportunities				4
42. Inform Mgmt. of Status of Team's Work			3 ⇒	
43. Fire Team Members				4
44. Develop Standards				4
45. New Product Development				4
46. Represent Team on Committees			3 ⇒	
47. Develop Criteria to Assess Team's Performance			3 ⇒	
48. Set Cost Reduction Targets				4
49. Develop Compensation Systems				4
50. Have Input on Hiring & Firing		2 ⇒		
51. Monitor Continuous Improvement				4
52. Continual Renewal/Redesign of Systems				4
53. Do Long-Range Planning				4

"*SAMPLE*" TRANSITION PLAN
STAGE I

Tasks/Responsibilities of Team:	Leaders Role *Coach* & Responsibilities:	Team Training Needed:
Decide on Goals for Team Cross-Train Team Members Schedule Vacations Select Team Leader (Leader Within Team) Decide Job Assignments Make Cost Improvements Make Quality Improvements Measure Team's Performance Schedule Work of Team Work with Internal Customers Maintain Safety & Housekeeping Motivate Team Members Define Areas of Team's Responsibility	Facilitate Team Meetings Determine Training Needs Schedule Training Coordinate with Team Leader/s Inside Team/s Build Group Into Team By: —Helping Members Get To Know & Trust Each Other —Facilitate Development of Team Mission, Goals, Ground Rules Provide Information Delegate Some Decisions Train/Teach Help Define Areas of Responsibility of Team Manage Boundaries: —Top Management —Other Teams/Shifts —Vendors —Support Groups —External Customers Conflict Resolution Prepare Reports Represent Team at Outside Meetings Do Performance Appraisal Technical Advisor	High-Performance: Definition; Roles & Responsibilities Communication Team Building Change Management Cross-Training Effective Meeting Skills Administrative Tasks Motivation Quality Tools, Measures, Concepts Customer Service Decision-making Problem-Solving State-of-the-Business

"*SAMPLE*" TRANSITION PLAN
STAGE II

Tasks/Responsibilities of Team:	Leader's Role & Responsibilities:	Team Training Needed:
Decide Resource Needs for Team Recognize Team Members for Superior Work Meet With Other Teams/Shifts Determine Training Needs Decide/Implement Process Improvements Input Engineering Changes Schedule Training Schedule Overtime Work with Vendors/Suppliers Keep Abreast of Goals & Objectives of Top Mgmt. Coach & Counsel Team Members Have Input on Hiring & Firing Team Members Facilitate Team Meetings	Continue to: Provide Information & Delegate Decisions Coach & Counsel Begin to Pull Back from Day-to-Day Matters Conflict Resolution Boundary Management Represent Team at Outside Meetings Monitor Individual Skill Development Monitor Progress of Team (Stages & Developmental Growth) Do Performance Appraisal (with peer input) Technical Advisor Co-Facilitate Team Meetings Teach Team to Prepare Reports Gather Input on Performance Appraisal	Coaching & Counseling Skills Cross-training Flow-Charting & Analyzing Work Processes Scheduling Vendor/Supplier Relations Role of Engineering Giving & Receiving Feedback Interviewing Skills Dealing with Conflict Diversity State-of-the-Business Time Management Leadership Skills Report Writing Facilitation Skills Reading Budgets Making Presentations Customer Service

"*SAMPLE*" TRANSITION PLAN
STAGE III

Tasks/Responsibilities of Team:	Leader's Role & Responsibilities:	Team Training Needed:

Hire New Team Members
Do Peer Appraisals
Represent Team at Outside Meetings
Represent Team on Committees & Task Forces
Monitor Individual Skill Development of Team Members
Develop Criteria to Assess Team Performance
Prepare Reports on Team's Progress on Goals
Secure & Distribute Resources
Resolve Personnel Issues Within Team
Inform Team of Other Teams' Needs
Align Team Goals with Individual Career Goals
Inform Mgmt. of Status of Team's Work
	Continue to: Provide Information & Delegate Decisions
	Teach/Train
	Pull Back from Day-to-Day Matters
	Manage Boundaries
	Spend More Time on Task Forces & Committees
	Do Long Range Planning
	Participate on & Facilitate Problem-Solving Groups
	Monitor Progress of Multiple Teams
	Technical Advisor
		EEO Laws
		Performance Appraisal Skills
		Project Management
		Cross-training
		Continue:
		    Cross-Training
		    Tech. Skills
		    Safety
		    Quality
		    State-of-the-Business
		Preparing Budgets

"*SAMPLE*" TRANSITION PLAN
STAGE IV

Tasks/Responsibilities of Team:	Leader's Role & Responsibilities	Team Training Needed:
Coordinating with Other Shifts & Teams Across the Site Monitoring Progress of Multiple Teams Preparing Budgets Identify New Business Opportunities Fire Team Members Develop Standards New Product Development Set Cost Targets Develop Compensation systems Monitor Continuous Improvement Work on Continual Renewal/Redesign of Systems Long-Range Planning	Transition to New Role: More Time with Committees, Task Forces, Problem-Solving Groups Technical Advisor Coach & Counsel Manage Boundaries New Role Options Are: Technical Expert to Several Teams Coordinator of Several Teams Faciliator Trainer Promotion to Newly Created Work Lateral Move to Other Part of Organization Just Starting or Expanding Teams	Continue: Technical Quality Customer Service State-of-the-Business Train-the-Trainer New Member Orientation Reward & Recognition Systems Career Development Lifelong, Continual Learning Work Redesign Process Improvement

HIGH-INVOLVEMENT EXERCISE:

Decision-Making

Learning Objective:

To discuss and reach consensus on which decisions your team is currently making; which decisions *should* the team be making, but isn't yet, and what will be needed to prepare the team for taking on these new decision-making responsibilities.

Directions:

Step One- Team Exercise

As a team, list the decisions your team is currently making. (5 min.)

_____   _____

_____   _____

_____   _____

_____   _____

Step Two- Team Exercise

Discuss, reach consensus,* and list the decisions the team *should* be making, but isn't yet. (15 min.)
*See "Guidelines for Reaching Consensus" on page 7.

_____   _____

_____   _____

_____   _____

_____   _____

Step Three- Team Exercise

Discuss, reach consensus,* and list all the information/training/resources the team will need before taking on these new decisions. (15 min.)
*See "*Guidelines for Reaching Consensus*" on page 7.

_____	_____
_____	_____
_____	_____
_____	_____
_____	_____
_____	_____
_____	_____

NOTES:

NOTES:

ACTION SEVEN

Building Work Groups Into "Teams"

- *High-Involvement Exercise: How Work Groups Are Different From Teams*
  - *Key Elements of High-Performing Teams*

- *Stages of Team Development*
  - *Stage I: Forming*
  - *Stage II: Storming*
  - *Stage III: Norming*
  - *Stage IV: Performing*

- *High-Involvement Exercise:*

  - *Developmental Needs At Each Stage*

  - *Preventing "Plateauing"*
    - *High-Involvement Exercise: Developing Your Team*
    - *Team Effectiveness Assessment*

111

HIGH-INVOLVEMENT EXERCISE:

How Work Groups Are Different from Teams

Learning Objective:

To understand the characteristics that differentiate teams from work groups.

Directions:

Step One- Individual Exercise

Think about the best "team" you've ever been a member of. Answer the following questions: (5 min.)

• What type of team was it? (sports team? work team?)

_____

• What characteristics made it the "best" team?

_____	_____
_____	_____
_____	_____
_____	_____
_____	_____
_____	_____
_____	_____
_____	_____
_____	_____

Step Two: Team Exercise

If you're doing this exercise with a team, discuss your lists and reach consensus* on a common list. (25 min.) (If you're *not* doing this exercise with a team, go on to "Step Three.")
*See *"Guidelines for Reaching Consensus"* on page 7.

Write your consensus list below:

_____

_____

_____

_____

_____

_____

_____

_____

_____

_____

Step Three- Team Exercise

Compare your list/s (individual & team) with the one on the following pages.

1. SHARED GOALS/MISSION Team members understand the goals because they have participated in setting them. There is a lot of discussion of the task and how to best accomplish it. Everyone feels a high degree of involvement. Each member feels that he/she makes a difference to the overall result.

2. A CLIMATE OF TRUST AND OPENNESS. The team creates a climate where members are comfortable and informal. Trust replaces fear and people are able and willing to take risks. It is a growth and learning climate where people are involved and interested.

3. OPEN AND HONEST COMMUNICATION. Team members feel free to express their thoughts, feelings, and ideas. Members listen to one another and everyone feels free to put forth an idea without being criticized or embarrassed. Conflict and disagreement are viewed as natural and dealt with. The team self-corrects by giving feedback to members on how they affect the team (positively or negatively) in meeting or not meeting its goals.

4. A SENSE OF BELONGING to the team and commitment to its actions. There is a sense of participation and a high-level of involvement. Out of this sense of inclusion ("I am an important part of this team and what I do makes a difference") comes high-commitment and pride in the team's accomplishments.

5. RESPECT FOR DIFFERENCES Team members view each other as unique people with valuable resources. Diversity of opinions, ideas, and experience is encouraged rather than practicing "Groupthink" where differences are viewed as deviating from the norm. Flexibility and sensitivity to others is practiced.

6. CONTINUOUS LEARNING/ IMPROVEMENT Team members are encouraged to take risks, and try something different. Mistakes are seen as part of learning through experimentation. Constant improvement can only take place if people are encouraged to try new ways and make suggestions on improvements without being punished.

7. ABILITY TO MEASURE & SELF-CORRECT. The team is able to constantly improve itself by examining its processes and practices. The team looks periodically at what may be interfering with its operations. Open discussion attempts to find the causes of problems whether they are procedures, individual behavior, etc. and the team develops solutions instead of letting problems worsen.

8. INTERDEPENDENCE Team members need one another's knowledge, skill, and resources to produce something together they could not do as well alone.

9. CONSENSUS DECISION-MAKING. Members of the team make decisions together that are of high-quality and have the acceptance and support of the entire team to carry them out.

10. PARTICIPATIVE LEADERSHIP. Whether the group has a designated leader or leadership shifts among the members, the leader does not dominate the group. Everyone is used as a resource.

The role of the leader is one of facilitator:

- Listening to Team Members
- Creating a Climate of Trust and Openness
- Eliminating Fear
- Valuing Diversity
- Role-Modeling ("Walking-the-Talk;" practicing what he or she preaches)
- Communicating the Goal and Mission of the Organization
- Delegating, Coaching, Counseling, and Teaching
- Encouraging Creativity, Risk-taking; and Constant Improvement of Everything by Everyone

- Sharing Information
- Motivating
- Empowering People (increasing their ability to do their job and serve the customer–better, faster, and with quality)
- Helping the Team become more and more self-directed (Less dependent on the Leader)
- Using Feedback to help the group self-correct by examining its procedures
- Dealing with Conflict
- Keeping the Team on Track
- Leading Effective Meetings
- Handling Personality Conflicts
- Developing the Team (by Understanding Group Dynamics)
- Managing Their Boss
- Influencing without Authority
- Breaking Down Cross-Functional Barriers

TEAM DEVELOPMENT

A common mistake we encounter in working with organizations is that although they say they want to create effective teams, they do not provide the team development necessary to build them. They make the mistaken assumption that people working in close proximity will automatically become teams as time goes by. Our experience has been that this is not true. Team development is a never-ending process. There are many skills that people need to learn or they will never reach their full potential as a team in terms of productivity and work satisfaction.

When high-performance succeeds, it is in environments where team development is actively pursued with time, money, training (formal and informal), books, videos, and other resources. In the long run this saves money and time that would otherwise be lost through costly trial and error mistakes. Also, work groups never achieve the synergistic breakthroughs (i.e., cost savings, time savings, quality improvements) of effective teams.

When we say "team development," we mean all of the following types of training:

- High-Performance—What it is and how it's different from traditional models
- Characteristics of Effective Teams
- Stages of Team Development
- Group Dynamics

- Interpersonal Skills: communication, active listening, conflict management, etc.
- Effective Meeting Skills
- Facilitation/Leadership Skills
- Problem-Solving
- Consensus Decision-Making

STAGES OF TEAM DEVELOPMENT

High-performing teams don't just happen, they require development over time. As work groups become teams, they go through inevitable, predictable stages. Just as human beings don't become adults until they first go through infancy, childhood, and adolescence, teams begin as groups of people and must go through stages before they become mature, effective teams. Since most groups never become teams and settle for less than they're capable of becoming, it's important to understand the stages and learn how to progress through them by addressing the developmental needs of each stage.

The following 4-stage model of team development is based on Tuckman's model of group development (1965) in which he summarized over fifty studies of group behavior. Each stage has unique characteristics which need to be understood in order to help groups move forward and not plateau.

STAGES OF TEAM DEVELOPMENT

Stage I: *"FORMING"* Team Characteristics:	Stage II: *"STORMING"* Team Characteristics:
• enthusiastic but skeptical • overwhelmed by all the newness • little or no commitment or trust • learning to get to know one another • not feeling any identity with the group • concerned about new roles & responsibilities • trying to cope with change & confusion • dependent on leaders • meetings tend to be long & unproductive, at first • struggling with making consensus decisions • overly polite & guarded • learning to problem-solve together • unsure of management's commitment to change effort • concerned about own competence in learning new skills • hopeful about the new opportunities & possibilities • developing mission & goals as a team • measuring work output/service	• becoming more "real" with one another & having more conflicts • getting to know & trust some, but not all, team members • learning what to do in crisis/emergency • "testing" the new systems & behaviors • struggling with taking ownership and not "fingerpointing" • "*unlearning*" attitudes & behaviors acquired over years • rivalry with other teams/shifts • a lot of complaining • struggling for power within team & with team leader • frustrated with learning new skills • surfacing problems & learning how to problem-solve together • learning to ask for help from team members • relying more on the team & less on leaders • taking on more responsibilities • clarifying roles • learning to examine group process & self-correct • facilitating own team meetings

Stage III: "*NORMING*" Team Characteristics:	Stage IV: "*PERFORMING*" Team Characteristics:
• striving for harmony • fact-based decision-making • living by ground rules • developing commitment to team • much more "business knowledge" • making more decisions (feeling empowered) • feeling of belonging to team • trust in team members • open & honest communication • giving & receiving peer feedback • learning to settle own conflicts without leader's intervention • taking on more leadership responsibility • members cross-trained in one another's work • beginning to plan ahead (more proactive than reactive) • listening to each other • breaking through barriers • feeling ownership of day-to-day responsibilities	• committed to team & total organization • collaborating with other teams/shifts • partnering with management • feeling like "owners" • measuring results & constantly improving • knowledgeable about customers & business • multi-skilled & flexible • more autonomy & self-direction • know what needs to be done & able to do it • rotate leadership duties among team members • team, individual, & organizational goals aligned with each other • able to anticipate customer needs • synergistic (team as a whole greater than the sum of the individual parts) • "smartening" the work & adding value • rewards tied to performance • willing to go above & beyond what's expected to accomplish goals (i.e., work overtime when needed) • able to make important decisions (i.e., hiring/firing team members, handling budgets, peer appraisal)

Based on the characteristics of teams at each of the four stages, let's next examine what teams need at each stage in order to grow and progress to the next stage:

DEVELOPMENTAL NEEDS DURING STAGES I & II:

■ Team Members need to get to know one another. Spend time learning about each member of the team: their likes & dislikes, strengths, weaknesses, career aspirations, backgrounds, what they'd like to learn, what motivates them, etc.

■ Teams need to discuss & reach agreement on ground rules for operating and decide on mission, & goals.

■ Teams need to be able to measure how they're doing (output, service, & team development).

■ Teams need to focus on their processes and not just the task itself. After analyzing their processes, they need to determine how to improve (self-correct).

■ A lot of communication is needed (talking/listening/dialoging).

■ Team Members need to agree on the climate they want to create in the group and commit to building it together.

■ Everyone needs to have patience and faith that the team will gel and productivity, which usually dips during this start-up phase due to all the new things to be learned, will eventually rise.

■ Conflict should be viewed as natural and should be dealt with by training team members in conflict management and agreeing on ground rules for addressing conflict.

■ Everyone needs to understand that trust does not develop overnight. Trust is built by sharing honest thoughts and feelings and developing clear expectations.

■ Top management needs to reassure everyone of their commitment (over-and-over) by communicating and "walking-the-talk."

■ Reading, visiting sites, attending workshops/conferences are all helpful.

■ During Stages I & II the organization plays a key role in turning crisis into opportunity by doing the following things:
  • Creating choices for people who will not work in teams. There will only be a few people who will not work in this new way and they will need to be given some choices. Usually, there are technical expert roles that they can fill.
  • Addressing the issue of job security is critical. People need to believe that gains in productivity will not cost them their job. Unless assurances like these are made, people will drag their feet, withhold ideas for improvements, and resist the change process. Job assurance does not mean a guarantee of lifetime employment. It usually takes the form of: Everyone's job will change, but no one will be out of work due to productivity gains.

DEVELOPMENTAL NEEDS DURING STAGE III:

■ Increase the team's knowledge of how the whole business works by supplying information and training.

■ Coordinate activities between teams and shifts that support interdependence rather than negative competition.

■ Management is learning new roles to support teams. Leaders need to pull back from the day-to-day involvement and let the teams manage the work. Leaders are then free to remove barriers, coordinate between teams, do long-range planning, and coach individual members.

Managers needs to fully understand this new concept and realize that unless they behave differently, nothing will change. Leaders need to give the work teams clear direction on *what* needs to be accomplished and autonomy and control over *how* they do the tasks. Teams need clear boundaries—they need to understand what they are and are not empowered to do.

■ As the team becomes less leader-centered and more able to make decisions and solve problems on its own, recognition and celebration of success is important to support further independence.

■ People will tend to revert to old ways of working. This regression and dependence on leaders is natural, but leaders need to avoid the temptation to act in the old ways and, instead, give team members the support and the training needed to take on more leadership, more responsibility, and ownership.

DEVELOPMENTAL NEEDS DURING STAGE IV:

■ Develop opportunities for team members to grow and develop

■ Revise appraisal and reward systems

■ Continue technical training

■ Measure, track and provide feedback so the team can self-correct

■ New goals need to be continually developed to challenge the teams (new products, new markets, new services, etc.)

■ Provide more information on business

■ Encourage new and innovative ideas

■ Empowered teams need never become stagnant, but should constantly find new ways to improve the work processes, the product/service (speed, cost, quality, etc.)

HIGH-INVOLVEMENT EXERCISE:

Stages of Team Development

Learning Objective:

To determine at which developmental stage your team is now and agree on what needs to be done to progress to the next stage.

Directions:

Step One- Individual Exercise (5 min.)

1. After reading the descriptions of the four developmental stages, which stage best describes where your team is now? Stage _____
    Reasons for choosing this stage?

    _____

    _____

2. What do you feel the team needs to do to move to the next stage? (If the team is already at Stage 4, what would continue to increase its growth and development?)

    _____

    _____

    _____

    _____

    _____

    _____

    _____

Step Two- Team Exercise

After discussing each individual's answers, reach consensus* on Questions #1 and #2. (15 min.)
*See *"Guidelines for Reaching Consensus"* on page 7.

The following actions/training will help our team move to the next stage & continue our growth & development:

_____

_____

_____

_____

_____

_____

_____

_____

_____

_____

_____

_____

_____

_____

_____

_____

_____

_____

_____

PREVENTING "PLATEAUING"

High-performing teams need the following things in order to keep growing, learning, & developing:

■ **INFORMATION** provided directly to the team on:
—Customer Requirements
—Safety
—Quality
—Finances
—Goals
—Performance Measures
—SPC
—Maintenance
—Vendors/Suppliers
—Quantity
—Materials/Tools/Machines
—Cost
—State of the Business

■ **EDUCATION/TRAINING/NEW SKILLS/KNOWLEDGE**
—Cross-Training
—Team Skills
—Leader/Coordinator Skills
—Interpersonal Skills
—High-performance Roles & Responsibilities

■ **DECISION-MAKING POWER** After teams have the necessary information and training, then everyone in the organization needs to push-down decisions. (This should be done gradually or the team will be overwhelmed.)

■ **REWARDS** need to be tied to improved performance (higher quality, lower costs, more quantity, faster cycle times, new skills learned, etc.)

HIGH-INVOLVEMENT EXERCISE:

Developing Your Team

Learning Objective:

To examine and agree on what your team needs for its continued development.

Directions:

Step One- Individual Exercise

Answer the following questions: (5 min.)

1. *What needed information is your team* not *getting at the present time?*

_____

_____

_____

_____

2. *What needed training is your team* <u>not</u> *getting at the present time?*

_____

_____

_____

_____

3. *Which decisions have been turned over to the team?*

_____

_____

_____

_____

4. Which decisions have <u>not</u> yet been turned over?

_____

_____

_____

_____

5. Have your reward/measurement/appraisal systems been revamped to support teams?

_____

_____

_____

_____

Step Two- Team Exercise

Discuss everyone's individual answers to each question and reach consensus* as a team. (20 min.)
*See "Guidelines for Reaching Consensus" on page 7.

1. _____

_____

2. _____

_____

3. _____

_____

4. _____

_____

5. _____

_____

HIGH-INVOLVEMENT EXERCISE:

Team Effectiveness Assessment

Learning Objective:

In order to continue developing, teams need to periodically assess themselves. The following assessment is designed to give your team an idea of how all the team members presently view the team.

Directions:

Step One- Individual Exercise (5–10 min.)

Circle the number that corresponds with your assessment of your team as it is now: 1 = Strongly Disagree; 2 = Disagree; 3 = Agree; 4 = Strongly Agree

1. Everyone on our team knows and agrees with the goals.   1 2 3 4

2. We measure how we're doing in quality, quantity, and customer service.   1 2 3 4

3. All our decisions are made by consensus.   1 2 3 4

4. Our leaders support us, give us resources, and empower us to make appropriate decisions.   1 2 3 4

5. Everyone on the team shares in the leadership duties.   1 2 3 4

6. We problem-solve and improve something every day.   1 2 3 4

7. We are open and honest with each other.   1 2 3 4

8. We dialogue about issues before we make decisions.   1 2 3 4

(*continued*)

9. Everyone on the team is seen as a valuable resource.   1 2 3 4

10. We take ownership and responsibility for completing tasks even if we have to come in early or stay late at times.   1 2 3 4

11. Our rewards are tied to performance.   1 2 3 4

12. Our team has a significant impact on the results we produce.   1 2 3 4

13. We are constantly provided with business information.   1 2 3 4

14. We are constantly learning new skills.   1 2 3 4

15. We use conflict constructively and do not avoid it.   1 2 3 4

16. We give each other accurate and timely feedback.   1 2 3 4

17. Team members have the skills necessary to perform the work.   1 2 3 4

18. Everyone knows and agrees on work priorities.   1 2 3 4

19. Everyone's role on the team is mutually agreed on.   1 2 3 4

20. Our goals are attainable.   1 2 3 4

21. We know and understand our mission.   1 2 3 4

22. We trust each other.   1 2 3 4

23. We are a highly productive team.   1 2 3 4

24. We have established ground rules we live by.   1 2 3 4

25. We are always more interested in learning from mistakes than placing blame.   1 2 3 4

Step Two- Individual Exercise

After everyone has completed their assessment, place your scores on the "Scoring Sheet" below, in the column marked "Individual Ratings." Then, total your individual ratings for each group of questions. (5–10 min.)

Step Three- Team Exercise

Average the scores for all team members by adding them together and dividing by the total number of members. Place these scores in the column marked, "Average of Team Member's Ratings" and total them for each group of questions. (10 min.)

SCORING SHEET

Team Mission & Goals	Ratings on Questions:					Totals:
	#1	#18	#19	#20	#21	
Individual's Ratings	__ +	__ +	__ +	__ +	__ =	_____ Total
Average of All Team Members' Ratings	__ +	__ +	__ +	__ +	__ =	_____ Total
Team Communication						
	#7	#8	#15	#16	#22	
Individual's Ratings	__ +	__ +	__ +	__ +	__ =	_____ Total
Average of All Team Members' Ratings	__ +	__ +	__ +	__ +	__ =	_____ Total

(*continued on next page*)

SCORING SHEET (*Continued*)

Team Behavior	Ratings on Questions:					Totals:
Individual's Ratings	#5 __ +	#6 __ +	#14 __ +	#24 __ +	#25 __ =	_____ Total
Average of All Team Members' Ratings	__ +	__ +	__ +	__ +	__ =	_____ Total
Team Productivity						
Individual's Ratings	#2 __ +	#10 __ +	#11 __ +	#12 __ +	#23 __ =	_____ Total
Average of All Team Members' Ratings	__ +	__ +	__ +	__ +	__ =	_____ Total
Team Empowerment						
Individual's Ratings	#3 __ +	#4 __ +	#9 __ +	#13 __ +	#17 __ =	_____ Total
Average of All Team Members' Ratings	__ +	__ +	__ +	__ +	__ =	_____ Total

Step Four- Team Exercise

Review your ratings for each of the five categories: "Team Mission & Goals," "Team Communication," "Team Behavior," "Team Productivity," "Team Empowerment"

Discuss and reach consensus* on what **actions** would increase your scores in each of the categories.
*See *"Guidelines for Reaching Consensus"* on page 7.

Team Mission & Goals:

_____

_____

_____

_____

Team Communication:

_____

_____

_____

_____

Team Behavior:

_____

_____

_____

_____

Team Productivity:

_____

_____

_____

_____

Team Empowerment:

_____

_____

_____

_____

NOTES:

NOTES:

ACTION EIGHT

Creating New Roles for Leaders

- *A New View of Leadership*
- *New Roles for Leaders in High-Performance Organizations*
- *Leadership Checklist*
- *Leadership Choices: Four Models*
- *Selecting a Team Leader*
- *The "New Role" of the Supervisor*
  - *Evolving from Supervisor to Team Coordinator*
- *Why Supervisors & Managers Resist Change?*
- *Changing Leadership Needs of Teams*
- *New Roles for Middle Managers*
- *High-Involvement Exercise: Choosing the <u>Best</u> Leadership Model*
- *My Leadership Style: A Self-Assessment*

135

CREATING NEW ROLES FOR LEADERS

A common misconception is that high-performing teams do *not* need leaders because teams can "self-manage." As a result of this myth, supervisors and managers are being fired, forced out, demoted, or set aside (told to turn over everything to the teams before the teams are ready).

While it is true that adults do not need to be "supervised" in the sense of being watched, controlled, or "bossed," leadership (supporting, coaching, inspiring, motivating, removing barriers, coordinating, training/teaching) is very much needed.

In fact, leadership is critical to building work groups into effective teams. The leader's role is extremely important in supplying what the team needs at each developmental stage so it will progress to the next stage, and eventually self-manage/self-direct. Even when the team has become high-performing, leadership will still be needed both inside the team (for coordinating among team members) and outside the team (for coordinating the boundaries between teams, shifts, support groups, customers, etc.)

Prior to implementation, the Steering Committee and Design Team (discussed during previous chapters) should rethink and redesign the role of leadership. This new definition should be consistent with the organization's new values, mission, and goals.

Key questions are: *"What kind of leadership is needed for our organization? What kind of leaders would best support our teams?"*

A NEW VIEW OF LEADERSHIP

Leadership in the traditional hierarchy *told* people what to do and *how* to do it. Money was seen as the prime motivator. Workers were not encouraged to change things. Decisions were made at the top and workers were expected to carry them out. *Thinking* and *doing* were separated.

Today's effective organization has turned the pyramid upside down. Now, customers are on top. Everyone is listening to the customer and acting on what they hear. Teams of workers are now empowered to do what needs to be done to satisfy the customer. Teams are constantly looking at what problems need to be solved, how costs can be lowered, waste and bureaucracy eliminated, things done faster, better, and smarter. Change is a constant.

Turning the pyramid upside-down requires a different state-of-mind on the part of leaders.

The following readings and exercises were created to provide information to enable you to rethink and recreate the leadership in your organization.

IMPORTANCE OF TEAM LEADERSHIP SUPPORTED BY RESEARCH:

According to a recent study of Self-Directed Work Teams,* there was a correlation between effective team leadership and positive results in terms of quality, productivity, and team member satisfaction. The following activities on the part of the supervisor or group leader were cited:

- Providing overall direction, resources, and business information to the teams
- Coaching teams to work together
- Recognizing the contributions made by the team

Self-Directed Teams: A Study of Current Practice, a joint study by AQP, DDI, & Industry Week Magazine.

Supervisors and managers need training in leadership skills in order to successfully transition from traditional to high-performance leaders.

NEW LEADERSHIP SKILLS NEEDED:

- Coordinating Teams, Shifts, etc.
- Team Building
- Facilitating Effective Team Meetings
- Facilitating Involvement & Participation
- Empowering Individuals & Teams
- Facilitating Team Problem-Solving
- Tapping "Synergy"
- Consensus-Decision-making
- Boundary Management
- Conflict Management
- Understanding Group Dynamics
- Teaching/Training
- Coaching/Counseling
- Managing Change
- Managing Diversity
- Communicating Mission & Goals
- Influencing Without Authority
- Building High-Performance, High-Involvement, & High-Commitment

EFFECTIVE LEADERS OF HIGH-PERFORMING TEAMS MUST HAVE THE FOLLOWING ATTITUDES & BELIEFS:

- People are the most valuable resource any company has.
- Human beings have unlimited potential to constantly grow, develop, and learn. Helping each team member achieve his/her potential is the main role of the leader.
- Leading a high-performing team is an art and a skill.
- Teams need constant developing.
- The leader's main job is listening to people not telling them what to do and how to do it. Workers are the "experts" on the work they do.
- The leader is there to be a resource to the teams by removing barriers, supplying tools, providing information, and asking, "What do you need?" "What can I do?"
- Everyone is capable of making decisions that affect them provided they are given the right information and training.
- The leader's role is one of teacher, coach, counselor, and trainer.
- People do not resist changes they have been in involved in making.
- Real employee involvement is a "process" not a "program."
- The leader's behavior must be consistent with self-direction beliefs (the leader is a role-model of the "new" way).
- The leader must be able to "let go" in order to empower people but not "dump" on people; train and coach them first so they'll be ready and able to succeed.
- In moving towards high-performance everyone's job changes and unless the leader changes, no one else will change.
- Realize mistakes are unavoidable. Help people learn from them.
- Don't shoot the messenger. All feedback is valuable.
- Recognize, reward, and celebrate the new behaviors.

NEW ROLES FOR LEADERS IN HIGH-PERFORMANCE ORGANIZATIONS

As traditional supervision gives way to self-directed/high-performing teams and organizations become flatter, leadership is still very much needed. The following list describes the kinds of leadership roles supervisors and managers evolve to as their old jobs change:

- **COORDINATOR**
  Linking the team with other teams and shifts; responsible for several teams

- **BOUNDARY MANAGER**
  Managing the boundaries between the teams, customers, vendors, functions, support groups, etc.

- **TRAINER/TEACHER/COACH/COUNSELOR**
  Helping team members learn all the new skills needed

- **FACILITATOR**
  Group process consultant; facilitating meetings and leading team building activities

- **CONFLICT MANAGER**
  Helping resolve conflicts between team members, between the team and other groups; teaching the team to manage conflict

- **TECHNICAL ADVISOR**
  Providing in-depth knowledge and expertise

- **MOTIVATOR/INSPIRATIONAL LEADER**
  Making sure team is focused on common vision, motivating everyone, encouraging, and recognizing both individual and team accomplishments

- **RESOURCE ALLOCATOR**
  Helping team manage resources and set priorities

- **EVALUATOR**
  Appraising performance (until team is ready to do it themselves)

- **COMMUNICATOR**
  Making sure the teams get pertinent information in a timely manner

- **INTRA-GROUP PROBLEM-SOLVING COORDINATOR/FACILITATOR**
  Bringing groups together who need to solve mutual problems

- **INNOVATOR**
  Focusing on trying new ways of doing things and encouraging risk-taking and innovation

- **LONG-RANGE, STRATEGIC PLANNER**
  Gathering and analyzing information on changing customer needs and market environment; working on goals and projects for future

In order to develop high-performing teams the role of leadership needs to be redesigned. Organizations generally do this in one of two ways: Some companies design teams where leadership shifts from member-to-member with no one person being "the leader" all the time. Other organizations designate a Team Leader (also called Group Leader, Facilitator, Resource, etc.) who is responsible for the leadership of the team. Exactly what the Team Leader is responsible for varies.

Let's examine what your Team Leader is responsible for. And if you don't have a designated Team Leader, who is responsible for this activity?

LEADERSHIP CHECKLIST

Instructions: **Place a check (✔) in column titled "Team Leader" next to the "Leadership Activities" your Team Leader is doing now.** If your team does not have one designated leader, write in column titled "Other" who is doing this now (i.e., team, managers)

Leadership Activities:	Team Leader	Other
Providing Overall Direction for the Team		
Providing Needed Business Information		
Coaching Team Members		
Facilitating Team Building Activities		
Recognizing Team Contributions		
Coordinating Between Teams/Shifts (Boundary Management; Linking)		
Coordinating With Support Groups		
Training		
Providing Technical Expertise		
Problem-solving Between Teams		
Conflict Management		
Providing Resources		
Evaluating Team Member's Performance		
Providing Inspiration (Leading by Example)		

(*continued*)

Leadership Activities:	Team Leader	Other
Championing Innovative Ideas		
Facilitating Team Meetings		
Budgeting		
Disciplining		
Hiring		
Firing		
Teaching Team to Measure & Evaluate Its Own Performance		
Fostering Continuous Improvement		
Teaching Quality Concepts		

QUESTIONS

After completing the "Leadership Checklist," discuss the following questions with your team. (20 min.)

1. *Are there important activities no one is doing?*

_____

_____

_____

_____

_____

2. *Are the right people doing the right things?*

_____

_____

_____

_____

_____

3. *Is there a transition plan to train team members to gradually assume more and more leadership tasks?*

_____

_____

_____

_____

_____

HIGH-INVOLVEMENT EXERCISE

Choosing the "*Best*" Leadership Model for Your Organization

In redesigning the role of leadership organizations must carefully select who is going to lead the work teams. Is it going to be:

- the former supervisor?
- one of the team members?
- a position rotated among all the team members?
- a transition role for the former supervisor?

Which is *best* for your organization? That depends on the following kinds of factors:

1. Where is your organization now in terms of its readiness for and commitment to high-performance?
2. What is the present relationship between supervisors and workers (participative or traditional)?
3. What career opportunities can be created for displaced supervisors and managers?
4. How could the talents of the current supervisors and managers best be utilized?

5. What form of leadership would best fit your organization's new values, vision, goals?
6. Which model would be easiest to implement?
   . . . cause the least disruption?
   . . . provide the best support to the teams?
   . . . prevent or lessen the dip in productivity that often accompanies the start-up of teams?
7. Which model do workers want most?
8. What support will be provided to the teams (training, coaching, etc.)?
9. What support will be provided to the team leaders (training, coaching, etc.)?

Keeping the above questions in mind, read the following pages which discuss the advantages and disadvantages of each leadership model.

(At the end of this section, pp. 164 & 165, this exercise will be continued.)

Leadership Choices:
Advantages & Disadvantages
of Four Leadership Models

Supervisor/Team Leader	Advantages:	Disadvantages:
Leader outside the team (Usually the former supervisor)	• Leader already in place, therefore, least disruptive choice • Taps supervisor's expertise on the work & knowledge of the people • Provides a trainer/teacher/coach, facilitator for team to rely on • Provides a key role for otherwise displaced supervisors • Provides team with an experienced leader • Support people, vendors, etc. continue to work with someone they know	• Runs risk of changing too little • Team members might tend to over-rely on the traditional leader & never self-direct • Must train the supervisor in the new skills needed • Past history ("old wounds") may not allow supervisor to change. (Could potentially be overcome by assigning supervisor to new team for a fresh start) • Supervisor may feel demoted (lacking former authority/status)

Leader Inside the Team	Advantages:	Disadvantages:
A team member who is sometimes paid more to also be team/group leader in addition to their regular work	• Team has opportunity to choose their leader • Shows a more dramatic shift in culture of the organization • A more democratic/ participative model • Team must rely on itself more & leadership less • Team members may choose a more participative type of leader • Team will help leader succeed because they have chosen him/her • Show's management's commitment to empowering the team • A working leader would understand more about team's needs	• Team may not choose the best person to lead the team (Sometimes management chooses the team leader for this reason) • Leader chosen may feel caught between being "liked" & doing what is in best interests of the organization • May cause rivalry among team members • May only recreate another "boss" • Requires training an inexperienced leader • More disruptive (more change to get used to) • Team may not be developmentally ready to make such an important decision • None of the team member's may want to be team leader

Rotating Team Leaders	Advantages:	Disadvantages:
Team members take turns being team leader. May use the "Star Model" where each team member represents the team at site-wide meetings & leads the team in certain areas, (i.e., quality, production, personnel, safety). Also called, shared team leadership	• Doesn't require extra money • Gives each team member an opportunity to lead • Develops everyone's leadership skills • Everyone understands & is skilled in the leadership tasks • Less likely that anyone will "boss" the team • Enhances everyone's sense of responsibility for team • Increases everyone's knowledge of the business • Enables team members to have contact with other teams, shifts, support groups, etc. across the site, therefore, increases sense of "one big company team" • Divides the leadership responsibilities into manageable parts • Most democratic & participative model	• Chaotic because people outside the team never know who the leader is at any given time and, therefore, don't know who to approach about a concern • Decision-making may be slower • In a crisis it is less clear who decides what to do (overcome by deciding & planning ahead of time) • Managers & support people will have more people with whom to coordinate • Not all team members will be equally skilled in leadership • Not all team members may want to be team leaders • Everyone will need leadership skills training • Requires a lot of coordination or it will be disruptive • Substitutes an experienced leader for inexperienced leaders

Transition Leader	Advantages:	Disadvantages:
Former supervisor remains team leader until team is ready to choose one team leader among themselves or rotate the leadership among the members	• Since the supervisor knows they're leaving, they can focus on teaching/training/coaching & not holding on to power • Utilizes supervisor's experience & abilities • Allows team to rely on the supervisor's leadership until the team is developmentally ready to take on the leadership themselves • Gives team a leader that will slowly, but surely, turn over everything to them (i.e., tasks and decisions) • Provides team with technical expert, coach, trainer, teacher, etc.	• Organization must decide what to do with the displaced supervisors (new roles must be created) • If supervisors are not given choices on their new roles, they may resist the change • Requires training for supervisors in new skills • Requires career development for supervisors & work security assurance so they will be willing to work themselves out of a job and transition to a new role

Since "shared leadership" is a less commonly known method, we thought it required some special explanation. We're not saying it's the "best" method, just that we think it should be considered and the following information will help you make an informed choice.

"SHARED" TEAM LEADERSHIP

Some organizations choose not to appoint one person as the team leader, but instead have the leadership duties rotate among all the members. Everyone has leadership duties in addition to their regular work. Leadership for the symbol points shifts among team members. For example, someone receives training in safety and for the next three months he/she attends all the plant-wide safety meetings as the team's representative. Then, someone else is trained in safety and takes over the role. In this way all team members develop their leadership abilities and have the opportunity to interact and coordinate with other teams.

The "Star Model"

By sharing leadership, team members enlarge their jobs to encompass many of the activities traditional supervision used to do. Companies doing this are learning that training is vital to making this work. So is coordination (making the time), and rewards need to be put in place to compensate people for taking on all the extra effort required.

Reasons for "Shared Leadership" Among Team Members

■ The organization does not want the team to rely on just one person as the leader, but rather develop everyone's leadership abilities.

■ The organization does not want the team to revert back to the traditional way of depending on "one" leader.

■ By sharing leadership the team is not leaderless; rather leadership shifts among team members who are responsible for various leadership functions. These duties vary with the nature of the work, but generally team members take responsibility for leading and coordinating efforts in these areas:

- Operations
- Training
- Safety
- Maintenance
- Scheduling
- Personnel/Administration
- Communication/Information
- Quality

Each Team Member is responsible for one of these areas (some teams appoint back-up people) for a designated period of time. Along with this leadership duty comes:

- Training to enable Team Members to handle the responsibility
- Responsibility to attend all site meetings dealing with the area and communicate back all vital information
- Commitment to represent the team

SELECTING A TEAM LEADER: DEVELOPING CRITERIA

If your team has been given the decision-making power to select a team leader, establishing criteria prior to selection is very important.

As you develop your criteria, consider the candidate's:

- technical expertise & skill level?
- relationships with other team members?
- relationships with managers?
- relationships with important others (i.e., support people & customers)?
- interspersonal skills (i.e., communication, listening, conflict management)?
- organization skills?
- facilitation skills?
- leadership abilities & demonstrated skills?
- level of commitment to the team concept?
- ability to learn?
- prior education & training?
- work habits (i.e., punctuality, absenteeism)?

- level of motivation?
- past work experience?
- "fit" with your organizational culture?
- Other criteria important to the team:

_____

_____

_____

_____

_____

_____

_____

Once the team has agreed on the criteria, agree on your method of selection: voting, consensus, ranking the criteria and rating each candidate, etc.

The form on the next page was designed to be used in the selection process. After your team has agreed on your criteria, fill in the blanks and rate each candidate on a scale from "1" (lowest) to "10" (highest) on each of the criteria.

Team Leader Selection Form

Name of Candidate ———————————————————————————

Name of Rater ———————————————————————————

Criteria:	Rating: (Scale of 1-10 1 = lowest 10 = highest)	Explanation:

THE "NEW ROLE" OF THE SUPERVISOR VS. TRADITIONAL SUPERVISION

Traditional Role of the Supervisor	New Role of the Supervisor*
• Reactive (spends time "fighting fires") • Expects a "fair day's work for a fair day's pay" • Makes decisions • Schedules the work • Passes down management's goals • Responsible for completing administrative paperwork • Evaluates people • Solves problems • Coordinates with other teams, shifts, support groups, etc. • Directs, controls, gives orders • Accountable & responsible for making sure employees do their work • Checks on employees • Involved in day-to-day tasks • Does all the planning, scheduling, etc. • Informs upper management of work progress • Passes down information he/she thinks the employees need to know • Resolves conflicts	• Proactive • Fosters "ownership" • Builds the team • Teaches team how to make effective consensus decisions • Teaches team to schedule, plan, etc. • Facilitates team in setting & achieving goals • Coordinates with other teams, shifts, support groups, vendors, suppliers, customers, etc. until team is able to do this • Teaches team to do administrative tasks (not all at once, but gradually) • Makes sure time is made for training • Trains/teaches • Provides information on all aspects of the business • Coaches & counsels • Enables team to do peer appraisal • Teaches team how to observe, understand, & improve group dynamics • Shares accountability & responsibility with team • Gradually pulls out of day-to-day (let's team handle that) & works on long-range projects • Teaches team how to facilitate team meetings

(*continued*)

*There is usually a change in title that corresponds to the new role, i.e., Team Leader, Coordinator, Coach.

Traditional Role of the Supervisor	New Role of the Supervisor
• Disciplines individuals • Manages one-on-one • Enforces work rules • Use fear as a motivator • Passes down upper management's rules & edicts whether or not he/she agrees with them	• Makes sure everyone participates • Teaches team to manage conflict • Trains the team in interviewing & selecting new members • Makes sure diversity is respected and valued • Teaches team to self-correct and continuously improve • Manages up • Models learning • Models good interpersonal skills

Many supervisors welcome the change in role because they have always done training, teaching, coaching, etc. As you can see from the long list, the new role means there's even more to do than before. Since so much rests on the frontline leader, he/she will need a lot of training, help, and support from the rest of the organization.

EVOLVING FROM SUPERVISOR TO TEAM COORDINATOR

The following model depicts the gradual transfer of responsibility and authority from the supervisor to the team itself. As this occurs everyone's role changes. As the team takes on more of the supervisor's old job, he/she is able to evolve to the new role.

Stage 1: (first 6 mos.)
Supervisor/Expert/Trainer

Leader at center of things. Behaving mostly as traditional supervisor, but supplying group with information, training in technical & administrative tasks, and gradually turning over responsibilities.

Stage 2: (first 12 to 18 mos.)
Coach/Advisor

Leader more on sidelines; stepping-in when needed to coach in building skills, give advice, breakdown barriers, etc.

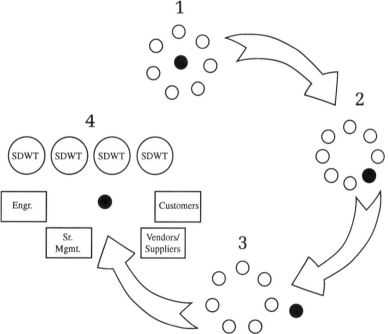

Stage 4: (after 2 yrs.)
Coordinator/Boundary Manager

Coordinating between several teams, shifts, vendors, customers. Planning his/her transition to next career step.

Stage 3: (after 1½ to 2 yrs.)
Resource/Facilitator

Expert on call; now free to do more long range planning, coordinating, etc. Lets the team handle day-to-day work.

WHY SUPERVISORS & MANAGERS RESIST CHANGE

Moving a traditional organization towards empowerment and high-performance means that everyone's job will change. This is particularly true for supervisors and middle managers who bear most of the burden for making these change efforts succeed.

The following reasons are often underlying causes of resistance:

- Supervisors & middle managers feel they must give-up things they like to do and are good at doing
- They lack the new skills needed (teaching, training, team development, coaching, etc.)
- They don't know if they're working themselves out of a job (or out of employment altogether)
- They don't know what their new roles will be
- They don't feel they have any choices

- They feel left out of the change process
- They have no sense of gaining anything to compensate for the losses
- They feel a loss of authority, prestige, status
- They have no career path or sense of advancement
- They're being asked to lead people & they don't know or agree with the direction
- They feel they're being taken out of the center of things and put on the sidelines
- They feel their expertise & experience are not given the credit they deserve
- They prefer the status quo
- They feel they're victims of unfair, incorrect assumptions about them (i.e., they're obsolete; they're too old to change)
- They're afraid they'll be fired as soon as the teams are successful
- They suspect the real motive behind all the changes is saving money by getting rid of supervisors/managers

ACTIONS FOR BUILDING COMMITMENT IN SUPERVISORS & MIDDLE MANAGERS:

Without the hard work and commitment of front-line leaders, change efforts have little chance of success. Supervisors and middle managers are needed to gradually build high-performing teams. The following actions will build commitment for a successful transition:

■ Assure supervisors & middle managers they will not lose their jobs even though their jobs will change

■ Train them in their new roles & help them develop new skills. They'll need training in:
  - New roles & responsibilities of high-performance
  - Coaching & counseling skills
  - Team development
  - Group dynamics
  - Interpersonal skills
  - Facilitation skills
  - Change management
  - Continuous improvement

■ Involve them in redesigning their current roles & designing new roles

■ Involve them in the total change effort

■ Give them choices & start training them for their new careers (technical expert to several teams, team coordinator, team leader, trainer, facilitator, etc.)

■ Have positive expectations (beware of negative self-fulfilling prophecies)

■ Listen to them (words & feelings)

■ Allow for mistakes

■ Don't "shoot the messenger"

■ Don't prejudge who will and who will not make this transition successfully

■ Be patient (commitment takes time to build)

■ Be a role model ("actions speak louder than words")

STAGES OF TEAM DEVELOPMENT

High-performing teams don't just happen, they require development over time. As work groups become teams, they go through inevitable, predictable stages. Just as human beings don't become adults until they first go through infancy, childhood, and adolescence, teams begin as groups of people and must go through stages before they become mature, effective teams. Since most groups never become teams and, thereby, settle for less than they're capable of becoming, it's important to understand the stages and learn how to evolve through them by addressing the developmental needs of each stage.

The following 4-stage model of team development is based on Tuckman's model of group development (1965) in which he summarized over fifty studies of group behavior. Each stage has certain unique characteristics which need to be understood in order to help groups move forward and not get "stuck" at an early stage. The following "Leadership Behaviors" will help work groups move forward and become effective teams.

STAGES OF TEAM DEVELOPMENT

Stage I: "Forming"	
Team Characteristics:	**Leadership Behaviors Needed:**
• enthusiastic but skeptical • overwhelmed by all the newness • little or no commitment or trust • learning to get to know each other • not feeling any identity with the group • concerned about new roles & responsibilities • trying to cope with change & confusion • dependent on leaders • meetings tend to be long & unproductive • struggling with making consensus decisions • overly polite & guarded • learning to problem-solve together • unsure of management's commitment to change effort • concerned about own competence in learning new skills • hopeful about the new opportunities & possibilities • developing mission & goals as a team • measuring work output/service	• build trust • help team members get to know one another • facilitate team meetings • keep team on target • teach team how to measure results & self-correct • teach team how to examine their processes (*how* they do things) • inspire • motivate • encourage • have faith the new system will work • direct/tell at first, until people know what to do • teach/train/guide • model good listening • provide information • be patient • help team develop goals, mission, & ground rules • be situational (modify leadership "style" to fit the task & the person)

Stage II: "Storming"	
Team Characteristics:	**Leadership Behaviors Needed:**
<ul><li>becoming more "real" with each other & having more conflicts</li><li>getting to know & trust each other</li><li>learning what to do in a crisis</li><li>struggling with not placing blame for mistakes</li><li>feeling closer to some team members, but not everyone</li><li>rivalry with other teams/shifts</li><li>a lot of complaining</li><li>struggle for power & control within team & with team leader</li><li>frustrated with learning new skills</li><li>surfacing problems & learning how to problem-solve together</li><li>taking on more responsibilities</li><li>taking on some of the leadership roles</li><li>learning to examine group process & self-correct/improve</li><li>facilitating team meetings</li><li>learning to ask for help from one another</li></ul>	<ul><li>teach team how to manage conflict</li><li>help team facilitate meetings</li><li>model open & honest communication</li><li>help team learn from mistakes & not place blame</li><li>encourage team to directly communicate with other teams, shifts, support groups, etc. & settle problems</li><li>coach individuals in technical & interpersonal skills</li><li>help everyone deal with frustration</li><li>observe & monitor group dynamics</li><li>make sure training takes place</li><li>continue to teach team members technical, interpersonal, & administrative skills</li><li>revisit team's goals, mission, & ground rules to make sure they're meaningful</li><li>foster interdependence</li></ul>

Stage III: "Norming"	
Team Characteristics:	**Leadership Behaviors Needed:**
<ul><li>striving for harmony</li><li>fact-based decision-making</li><li>living by ground rules</li><li>developing commitment to team</li><li>much more "business" knowledge</li><li>making more decisions (feeling empowered)</li><li>feeling of belonging to team</li><li>trust in team members</li><li>open & honest communication</li><li>giving & receiving peer feedback</li><li>learning to settle own conflicts without leader's intervention</li><li>taking on more leadership responsibility</li><li>members cross-trained in one another's work</li><li>beginning to plan ahead (more proactive than reactive)</li><li>listening to each other</li><li>breaking through barriers</li><li>feeling ownership of day-to-day responsibilities</li></ul>	<ul><li>able to pull back from day-to-day tasks</li><li>more focused on "big picture"</li><li>more boundary management with customers, suppliers, vendors, & upper management</li><li>taking on new tasks that used to be done by higher levels of management</li><li>still there for team, but more as resource, technical expert-on-call, etc.</li><li>considering new role options as team takes on more & more of the old role</li></ul>

Stage IV: "Performing"	
Team Characteristics:	**Leadership Behaviors Needed:**
• committed to team & total organization • collaborating with other shifts & teams • partnering with management • feeling like "owners" • measuring results & constantly improving • knowledgeable about customers & business • more autonomy & self-direction • know what needs to be done & able to do it • rotating leadership duties among team members • team, individual, & organizational goals aligned • multi-skilled & flexible • able to anticipate customer needs • synergistic (team more effective together than as individuals) • "smartening" the work by adding value • rewards tied to performance • willing to go above & beyond what's expected to accomplish goals (i.e., work overtime) • able to make important decisions: hiring/firing team members, budgets, peer appraisal, etc.	• concerned more with needs of overall business • providing resources for team • coordinating between several teams, shifts, support groups, customers, vendors, suppliers, etc. • beginning new role: coordinator of many teams, technical expert to several teams, trainer/facilitator, working with new teams just starting the process, working in new department/division, etc.

NEW ROLES FOR MIDDLE MANAGERS

- Managing constant change
- Sponsoring/coaching teams
- Developing an overall transition plan
- Championing innovative ideas
- Managing the boundaries between teams & the rest of the organization, customers, vendors, suppliers, etc.
- Providing resources
- Focusing on goals & results
- Breaking down barriers that are getting in the way of the teams performance
- Keeping-up with technological changes & market trends
- Making process improvements
- Championing continuous improvement
- Role modeling the "new" way
- Building trust
- Communicating
- Involving everyone
- Monitoring how decisions are made & by whom (i.e., making sure consensus decisions have true consensus)
- Valuing & managing diversity
- Creating recognition & pay-for-performance systems
- Making sure there's cross-functional alignment
- Pushing-down accountability for business results
- Providing business information
- Reinforcing the new values
- Making sure everyone is involved in achieving the organization's goals
- Measuring success
- Developing new products
- Creating career opportunities in the flatter organization
- Balancing all the various change efforts & unifying them
- Partnering with employees, the union, customers, vendors, suppliers, etc.

Managers play a key role in giving the work teams clear direction on "what" needs to be accomplished and autonomy and control over "how" they do the tasks. Teams need managers to provide business information and set the boundaries on what the teams are and are *not* empowered to do.

As the organization moves towards high-performance, leaders at all levels "download" some of their responsibilities to the next level so everyone is empowered with high-level work and decision-making power. As the teams take on more and more of the day-to-day responsibilities, the next level of management is free to do work the level above them used to do, and so on. This enables managers to have more time to do long range strategic planning, initiate process improvements, and other actions that needn't be left on the "back burner" any longer.

HIGH-INVOLVEMENT EXERCISE

Choosing the *Best* Leadership Model for Your Organization

Learning Objective:

To help individuals and teams think through, discuss, and agree on what would be the "best" leadership model for their organization.

Directions:

After reading this section, we'd like to return to the questions posed on page 144.

Step One- Individual Exercise

Answer the following questions about your current organization. (10 min.)

1. .Where is your organization now in terms of its readiness for, and commitment to, high-performance?

_____

_____

2. What is the nature of the present relationship between supervisors and workers (participative or traditional)?

_____

_____

3. What career opportunities can be created for displaced supervisors? managers?

_____

_____

4. How could the talents of the current supervisors and managers best be utilized?

_____

_____

5. What leadership model will best fit your organization's new values, vision, goals?

    _____

6. Which model would be the easiest to implement? _____

    . . . cause the least disruption? _____

    . . . provide the best support to the teams? _____

    . . . prevent or lessen a dip in productivity? _____

7. Which model do workers most want? _____

8. What support will be provided to the teams (training, coaching, etc.)?

    _____

9. What support will be provided to the leaders (training, coaching, etc.)?

    _____

10. Other factors to consider?

    _____

    _____

    _____

    _____

    _____

Step Two- Team Exercise

Discuss your answers to the questions 1–10 and then reach consensus* on which of the four leadership models (Supervisor/Team Leader, Leader Inside the Team, Rotating Team Leaders, Transition Leader) would best suit your organization at this time. (20 min.)
*See "*Guidelines for Reaching Consensus*" on page 7.

Write the team's choice here:

_____

Explain rationale for choice:

_____

_____

_____

_____

_____

_____

_____

MY LEADERSHIP STYLE: A SELF-ASSESSMENT

Directions: Rate your present Leadership Style by indicating whether you do this: "Always," "Most of the Time," "Some of the Time," "Rarely"

As a Leader I: (Circle Your Answer- 1, 2, 3, or 4)	Always	Most of the Time	Some of the Time	Rarely
1. Get to know each member of the team.	4	3	2	1
2. Listen more than I talk.	4	3	2	1
3. Help the team stay on target.	4	3	2	1
4. Remove barriers that get in the team's way.	4	3	2	1
5. Use consensus decision-making.	4	3	2	1
6. Help the team set & achieve goals.	4	3	2	1
7. Recognize team members accomplishments and give positive feedback.	4	3	2	1
8. Help the team resolve conflicts.	4	3	2	1
9. Share business information with team.	4	3	2	1
10. Use mistakes as learning opportunities.	4	3	2	1
11. Encourage open & honest communication.	4	3	2	1
12. Actively build the team.	4	3	2	1
13. Coach & counsel team members.	4	3	2	1
14. Celebrate team accomplishments.	4	3	2	1
15. Help the team measure & self-correct.	4	3	2	1
16. Train team members.	4	3	2	1
17. Facilitate team meetings.	4	3	2	1
18. Coordinate between team & other teams, shifts, etc.	4	3	2	1
19. Encourage ideas and suggestions from team members and act on them.	4	3	2	1
20. Inform people outside our team of what we're doing.	4	3	2	1
21. Facilitate the team in identifying and solving work-related problems.	4	3	2	1
22. Respect & value diversity.	4	3	2	1
23. Facilitate the team in constantly learning and changing.	4	3	2	1
24. Listen to our customers (internal and external).	4	3	2	1
25. See my behavior as role-modeling for the team.	4	3	2	1

ACTION COMMITMENTS:

Based on this Self-Assessment of my "Leadership Style," these are the actions I'm committed to taking:

_____

_____

_____

_____

_____

_____

_____

_____

_____

_____

_____

_____

_____

Note: My Leadership Style "Self-Assessment" could also be used to gain feedback on your leadership style from the team members. Give each member a copy and have them assess you after a specific meeting or on your general leadership. Responses should be anonymous. This can be most helpful if your attitude as the leader is that _all_ feedback is good because it's valuable information you can use.

NOTES:

NOTES:

ACTION NINE

Training! Training! Training!

- *Towards a Learning Organization*
- *Three Types of Training Needed by Team Members*
- *Training Needed by Leaders*
- *Training Teams Need During the Four Developmental Stages*
- *Developing a "Just-In-Time" Training Plan*
- *High-Involvement Training Activities For Team Members & Team Leaders:*

(continued)

TRAINING ACTIVITY #1: Setting Ground Rules

TRAINING ACTIVITY #2: Establishing Norms

TRAINING ACTIVITY #3: Characteristics of an Effective Team Member

TRAINING ACTIVITY #4: Self-Assessment-How Do You Rate As A Team Member?

TRAINING ACTIVITY #5: Importance of Team Meetings
- *Team Meeting Assessment*
- *Actions to Facilitate "Positive" Dynamics*

TRAINING ACTIVITY #6: Developing "Active" Listening Skills
- *Why Listening is the #1 Skill of an Effective Team Member*
- *What Does an "Active Listener" Do?*
- *Listening Self-Assessment*
- *Why Effective Listening Is Good Business*
- *The Importance of Listening to Leading/ Facilitating a Team*

TRAINING ACTIVITY #7: Developing Coaching Skills
- *Brainstorming Session on "Qualities of Good Coaches"*
- *Conducting an Effective Coaching Session*

TOWARDS A LEARNING ORGANIZATION

We've emphasized training in our action title because it would be impossible to overstate how important it is to the success of change efforts. Empowerment, involvement, high-performance, and continuous improvement all depend on informed/trained people.

One of the main reasons we've fallen behind in American organizations is that we don't do enough training. The following statistics,* based on recent research, bears this out:

- Only 11% of American workers receive formal training from their employers
- More than 80% of U.S. employers do no training at all
- Most training in America now goes to white-collar, technical, and executive people not frontline employees whose actions directly produce products and services
- The best U.S. companies spend 3%–7% of their payroll on training
- Productivity returns on training are three times its costs
- Only 13% of American employers have organized into high-performance work systems (a mere 2% of U.S. workers)

- 40% of business improvements come through buying machinery; 60% has to be learned at work. Without proper training we will have new technology, but will not have the trained people who can maximize its potential.

These statistics support one of the most significant paradigm shifts today:

In high-performance organizations *all* employees need training because everyone is important to the total process and everyone is capable of "smartening" the work.

The successful competitor will be the one who produces the product or delivers the service the quickest, with the highest quality, and the lowest cost (just one of these isn't good enough anymore). This is a very lofty goal and it can only be accomplished by organizations that are lean, agile, and have trained, knowledgeable, and committed workers.

How long do we train people? FOREVER! Continuous improvement comes from investing in people by providing opportunities for everyone to constantly learn.

*"What Training Means in an Election Year," *Training & Development Magazine,* 1992.

TRAINING NEEDED BY LEADERS

Team leaders, supervisors, and managers will need the following types of training in order to understand their new roles and develop skills in leading teams:

- What is high-performance? (new values & attitudes)
- New roles & responsibilities of team members & team leaders
- Communication (esp. listening)
- Facilitation
- Diversity
- Problem-solving
- Consensus decision-making
- Group dynamics
- Effective meetings
- Coaching & counseling
- Conflict management
- Giving & receiving feedback
- Change management
- Participative leadership

THREE TYPES OF TRAINING
NEEDED BY TEAM MEMBERS

1—High-Performance Training

Everyone will need training in what high-performance means, how it's different from traditional organizations, and how everyone's role will have to change. Team members and leaders will also need training in team skills: communication (especially, listening), problem-solving, decision-making, team building, group dynamics, effective meetings, conflict resolution, etc.)

2—Technical Skills Training

This will vary depending on the specific work of the team. Much of this will be done by team members cross-training one another so everyone becomes "multi-skilled" and able to perform one another's jobs. Teams will also need quality and safety training.

3—Administrative Training

Much of the administrative work of traditional supervision can and should be performed by the team members themselves so leaders can do other things to support the team. This training should be done gradually so the team does not feel overwhelmed. It is best to begin with easier tasks or decisions first and more difficult ones after the team has had some experience and success. Vacation scheduling is usually an easy decision while appraisal is more sensitive and difficult. The correct sequence is to first give the team information, then training, and lastly, delegate the task.

TRAINING TEAMS NEED DURING
THE FOUR DEVELOPMENTAL STAGES

In "Action Seven: Developing Work Groups Into Teams," the four developmental stages were described. Teams need training at each stage to help them progress to the next stage and not plateau.

Each organization must decide what specific training is needed. The following generic sample serves as an example in aiding you in creating your own unique, custom-designed training plan.

STAGES OF TEAM DEVELOPMENT

Stage I: *"FORMING"* Team Characteristics:	Stage II: *"STORMING"* Team Characteristics:
• enthusiastic but skeptical • overwhelmed by all the newness • little or no commitment or trust • learning to get to know each other • not feeling any group identity • concerned about new roles & responsibilities • trying to cope with change & confusion • dependent on leaders • meetings tend to be long & unproductive, at first • struggling with making consensus decisions • overly polite & guarded • unsure of management's commitment to change effort • concerned about own competence in learning new skills • hopeful about new opportunities • developing team mission & goals • measuring work output/service	• becoming more "real" with each other & having more conflicts • getting to know & trust some, but not all, team members • learning what to do in crisis/ emergency • "testing" the new systems • struggling with taking ownership and not "fingerpointing" • "unlearning" attitudes & behaviors • rivalry with other teams/shifts • a lot of complaining • struggling for power within team & with team leader • frustrated with learning new skills • surfacing problems & learning how to problem-solve together • learning to ask one another for help • relying more on one another & less on leaders • taking on more responsibilities • clarifying roles • learning to examine group process • facilitating own team meetings

Stage I: Training:	Stage II: Training:
• Cross-training ----------------------------- on-going --------------------------------------- • Communication • High-performance concepts, roles, & responsibilities • Team Development ---------------------- on-going -------------------------------------- • Problem-solving • Consensus decision-making • Effective meetings • Technical training ------------------------- on-going --------------------------------- • Quality concepts & tools ----------------- on-going ------------------------------- • Safety --- on-going ---------------------------------	• Dealing with conflict • Diversity • Benchmarking with successful cos. • Administrative skills -------------------- • Leadership skills • Facilitation skills

Stage III: *"NORMING"* Team Characteristics:	Stage IV: *"PERFORMING"* Team Characteristics:
• striving for harmony • fact-based decision-making • living by ground rules • developing commitment to team • much more "business" knowledge • making more decisions (feeling empowered) • feeling of belonging to team • trusting in team members • open & honest communication • giving & receiving peer feedback • learning to settle own conflicts without leader's intervention • taking on more leadership responsibility • members cross-trained in one another's work • beginning to plan ahead (more proactive than reactive) • listening to each other • breaking through barriers • feeling ownership of day-to-day responsibilities	• committed to team & company • collaborating with other teams • partnering with management • feeling like "owners" • measuring results & constantly improving • knowledgeable about customers & total business • multi-skilled & flexible • knowing what needs to be done & able to do it • rotating leadership duties among team members • team, individual, & organization goals aligned with each other • able to anticipate customer needs • synergistic • "smartening" the work & adding value • rewards tied to performance • willing to go above & beyond what's expected to accomplish goals • able to make important decisions

Stage III: Training:	Stage IV: Training:
--- on-going ---→	
• Coaching & counseling ----------------- on-going ---→	
• Interviewing • Feedback & appraisal	• Hiring & firing • Peer review
--- on-going ---→	
--- on-going ---→	
• Budgeting	• Strategic, financial, tactical knowledge of business
--- on-going ---→	
--- on-going ---→	
--- on-going ---→	

HIGH-INVOLVEMENT EXERCISE

Training for High-Performance

Learning Objective:

To help individuals and teams determine at which stage their team is currently and agree on the training needed to evolve to the next stage.

Directions:

Step One- Individual Exercise

After reading the preceding pages describing the four stages, decide at which stage your team is now. (5 min.) Stage _____
(Explain answer.)

_____

_____

Step Two- Team Exercise

Discuss your individual answers with the team and reach consensus* on which stage the team is now. (20 min.) Stage _____
(Explain answer.)

_____

_____

Step Three- Team Exercise

Discuss and reach consensus* on the training needed to move your team forward to the next stage of development. (15 min.)

_____

_____

_____

_____

*See "Guidelines for Reaching Consensus" on page 7.

HIGH-INVOLVEMENT EXERCISE

Developing a "Just-In-Time" Training Plan

Learning Objective:

To determine the training team members have already received before planning additional training.

Directions:

Step One- Individual Exercise

Ask each team member to complete the first column, "Training Received." (5 min.) (The second column will be completed after the training transition plan has been developed.)

Types of Training Teams Need	Training Received (✔)	Training Planned (Date)
New Roles & Responsibilities in High-Performance		
Problem-Solving Skills		
Quality Concepts		
Using Quality Tools		
Work Flow Process Analysis		
Presentation Skills		
Understanding Group Dynamics		
Budgeting		
Selecting Team Members (Interviewing)		
Decision-making Skills		
Communication Skills		
Conflict Management		

(continued)

Types of Training Teams Need	Training Received (✔)	Training Planned (Date)
Measuring & Evaluating Team Performance		
Effective Meeting Skills		
Technical Skills (includes Cross-Training)		
Diversity		
Leadership Skills		
Facilitation Skills		
Safety		

Step Two- Team Exercise

After compiling the data on who has already received training in the various areas, determine *what* training needs to be done and *when* it should occur. (We're calling this "just-in-time" training because usability should be a prime consideration. For example, if a team is going to hire a new team member, interviewing skills training must be done first. If a team is *not* going to be hiring anyone in the near future, then interviewing skills training would not be necessary. It should first be determined what skills are going to be needed prior to start-up, first six months, next six months, and so on.) (30 min.)

J-I-T TRAINING PLAN

	Prior To Start-Up	Stage I First 6 mos.	Stage II Next 6 mos.	Stage III After 1 yr.	Stage IV After 2 yrs.
TEAM MEMBERS					
TEAM LEADERS					
TEAM MANAGERS					

TRAINING ACTIVITY #1:

Setting Team Ground Rules

Learning Objective:

One of the first things a new team needs to do is discuss and agree on its ground rules so it can operate with maximum efficiency.

Directions:

Step One- Individual Task

Read each statement and indicate whether you *agree* or *disagree* with it by placing an "A" in the parenthesis or a "D."

Key: "A" if you agree; "D" if you disagree.

(   ) 1. A primary concern of all team members should be to establish an atmosphere where all are free to express their opinions.

(   ) 2. In a team with a strong leader, an individual is able to achieve greater personal security than in a team with a more passive leader.

(   ) 3. There are often occasions when an individual who is part of a working team should do what he/she thinks is right regardless of what the group has decided to do.

(   ) 4. Members should be required to attend team meetings.

(   ) 5. Generally, there comes a time when democratic group methods must be abandoned in order to solve practical problems.

(   ) 6. In the long run, it is more important to use participative methods than to achieve specific results by other means.

(   ) 7. Sometimes it is necessary to change people in the direction you yourself think is right, even when they object.

(   ) 8. It is sometimes necessary to ignore the feelings of others in order to reach a group decision.

(   ) 9. When leaders are doing their best, one should not openly criticize or find fault with their conduct.

( ) 10. Meetings would be more productive if the leader would get quickly to the point and say what he/she wants the group to do.

( ) 11. Conflict among team members should be avoided.

( ) 12. Interest falls off when everybody in the group has to be considered before making decisions.

( ) 13. Teamwork increases when the leader is careful to choose friends as team members.

( ) 14. A team is no stronger than its weakest member.

( ) 15. In the long run, it is more productive to replace an ineffective team member than to try and retrain him/her.

( ) 16. Once a team gets established in a set way of working, it is almost impossible to change.

( ) 17. When a team gets a new leader, the whole pattern of the team changes.

( ) 18. One resistant team member can keep a whole team from improving its performance.

( ) 19. The most important condition in a successful team building program is the motivation level of the team members to want to see the program succeed.

( ) 20. To become a really effective team, members should have a personal liking for each other.

( ) 21. A team decision is always better than an individual decision.

Step Two- Team Exercise

When everyone is finished, discuss your individual answers and then reach consensus* on whether you agree or disagree with each statement. (You can all agree, disagree, or change the wording in order to reach consensus.) (35 min.)
*See "Guidelines for Reaching Consensus" on page 7.

Step Three- Team Exercise

Read and discuss the following two pages:

The statements you just discussed are good vehicles for getting to know one another and the opinions that make you unique. Everyone's opinion needs to be heard. You probably learned that in many cases even your definitions of words were different. You probably had to change some wording in order to finally agree, and in the process you might have come out with a statement that is even better than the original one.

Every team needs to engage in the process of establishing its own ground rules (mutually agreed ways of conducting itself). Teams will vary in this because the people are different and in many ways the rules don't matter as long as the team members agree on them.

The process of reaching consensus on these matters is very important (in other words, *how* you do it is as critical as the results). Each person needs to be listened to. If some members are quiet, they need to be drawn out. If other people are exerting too much influence, they need to listen more and talk less.

The final results of consensus will not be that everyone agrees 100%, but rather they feel heard, can live with the ground rules, and will support them. If anyone cannot, or will not, support the final results—the team isn't finished and must talk more. Ground rules are meaningless unless all team members buy into and live them.

THE PURPOSE OF TEAM GROUND RULES

- To express the values of the Team

- To make sure every Team Member knows and agrees with what's expected of him or her

- To develop norms that support the needs of the Team Members and the needs of the organization

- To help the Team evaluate its performance

- To help orient a new Team Member so he or she will know the team's expectations

- To have everyone agree on what's important to the Team and provide a guide for behavior

A new team needs to discuss and decide on ground rules for issues like these:

1. How often shall we hold team meetings?
   - How long should they be? When? Where?
   - How should we establish the agenda?
   - Who is going to chair the meetings? Take minutes?
2. How are we going to get feedback and measure our performance?
3. What is our goal/purpose as a team?
4. How can we best accomplish our mission? What ground rules do we all agree would help us accomplish our goals?
5. What are our expectations for the team? (Each of our biggest worries? Hopes? Past experiences with teams?)
6. How will we make decisions?
7. How will we resolve problems and handle conflicts?
8. How do we make sure everyone is listened to and everyone has a say?
9. How will we handle time constraints?
10. How will we prioritize our work?
11. How will we measure our productivity? Quality?
12. How will we self-correct (look at what we're doing and make corrections)?
13. What kind of climate do we want in our group? How can we build the kind of climate we want?
14. How can we constantly improve what we do?
15. What skills do members have and which do they want to learn? How are we going to build cross-training into our schedule?
16. What other kinds of operating guidelines do we need to formulate? (attendance, tardiness, vacation, scheduling, etc.)

_____

_____

_____

_____

_____

_____

_____

_____

Step Four- Individual Exercise

As you think about this team, write down one ground rule you think is important to its effectiveness, productivity, teamwork, work satisfaction, etc. (5 min.)

_____

_____

Step Five- Team Exercise

When everyone has finished "Step Four," write everyone's ground rules here:

1. _____
2. _____
3. _____
4. _____
5. _____
6. _____
7. _____
8. _____
9. _____
10. _____
11. _____
12. _____
13. _____
14. _____
15. _____

Step Six- Team Exercise

Discuss the entire list of everyone's ground rules (eliminating or changing any item). Reach consensus* on the ones the team wants to adopt as its ground rules. (List your final ground rules on the next page and post in a prominent place.)
*See "_Guidelines for Reaching Consensus_" on page 7.

Our Team's Ground Rules:

_____

_____

_____

_____

_____

_____

_____

_____

_____

_____

_____

_____

_____

_____

_____

_____

_____

_____

_____

_____

OUR TEAM'S GROUND RULES (AN EXAMPLE)

1. Team meetings will be attended by all team members:
   - we'll begin & end on time
   - we'll meet once a week for one hour
2. We will treat each other with respect:
   - listen to each other
   - communicate openly & honestly
   - keep confidences "confidential"
   - respect and value our diversity
   - settle our problems; handle our conflicts
   - continue to build trust
3. We will always place our customers first.
4. We will agree on goals together.
5. We will measure how we're doing (output, quality, customer service, etc.) and pursue continuous improvement.
6. We will work together as a team to keep improving our work and build our team.
7. We will cross-train one another:
   - coach one another
   - communicate needed information
   - solve problems together
8. We will cooperate with and support other teams.
9. We will have a team rep (a rotating position) meet with the next shift for 15 minutes each day.
10. We will make decisions together on the basis of consensus.
11. We will share the leadership duties for team meetings and administrative tasks.
12. We will support team leaders.
13. We will encourage new ideas, suggestions, etc. from everyone and try new and better ways of doing things.
14. We will continue to grow, develop, and learn as individuals and as a team.
15. We will orient new members and get their input on these ground rules.
16. We will periodically revisit these ground rules to make sure we're living up to them and change or revise them accordingly.

TRAINING ACTIVITY #2:

Examining Team Norms

Learning Objective:

To discuss and agree on the team's operating norms and their impact. To enable a team to examine and change the norms that are having a negative impact.

Directions:

What a group agrees on is a ground rule; what actually happens is a norm. Unlike ground rules, norms are _unwritten_ rules of behavior which impact how we work together. All groups have norms, but usually these norms are not discussed and so are never examined.

Step One- Team Exercise

As a team brainstorm* the norms you have as a team. (10 min.) (_Write them in the column on the left._)
*"Guidelines for Brainstorming" on page 26.

Norm:	Impact:
Example: Our meetings start on time.	_Some members miss the first few minutes._

Step Two- Team Exercise

After the team has completed the list of norms, discuss and reach consensus** on which ones are truly your norms. (10 min.)
**See _"Guidelines for Reaching Consensus"_ on page 7.

Step Three- Team Exercise

Reach consensus and list, in the column to the right, the "Impact" of each norm. (15 min.)

Step Four- Team Exercise

After you've reached agreement on your final list of norms, answer the following questions: (15 min.)

1. *How do these norms agree or disagree with our stated ground rules?*

    _____

    _____

    _____

    _____

2. *Which norms do we want to change? Why?*

    Norm _____

    Reason for Changing _____

    Norm _____

    Reason for Changing _____

    Norm _____

    Reason for Changing _____

3. *Any other thoughts concerning team norms or ground rules?*

    _____

    _____

    _____

    _____

    _____

    _____

TRAINING ACTIVITY #3:

Characteristics of An Effective Team Member

Learning Objective:

To discuss and agree on the characteristics which constitute an effective team member.

Directions:

Step One- Individual Exercise

Think about the best team you've ever been a member of. Answer the following questions: (5 min.)

1. What type of team was it? _____

2. What made it the best team? _____

_____

_____

3. What were the characteristics of the team members? Of course, they were all unique people, but, generally, what traits made them good team members? List them below:

_____   _____

_____   _____

_____   _____

_____   _____

_____   _____

_____   _____

Step Two- Team Exercise

After discussing each individual's list, reach consensus* on a list of characteristics of a good team member of *this* team. What qualities do you want the people on your team to develop so they'll be good, effective team members? (25 min.)
*See *"Guidelines for Reaching Consensus"* on page 7.

CHARACTERISTICS OF AN EFFECTIVE MEMBER
OF OUR TEAM:

_____

_____

_____

_____

_____

_____

_____

_____

_____

_____

_____

_____

_____

_____

_____

_____

_____

_____

_____

Step Three- Team Exercise

Read and discuss the following list with your team. How does it compare with your list? (10 min.)

AN EFFECTIVE TEAM MEMBER:

- Understands the importance of listening & demonstrates active listening skills
- Demonstrates commitment to the team (i.e., is present & punctual at meetings)
- Communicates openly & honestly
- Works through conflict; doesn't avoid it
- Is always learning & improving
- Is open to new & better ways of doing things
- Strives to improve results, processes, etc.
- Asks for & gives feedback
- Utilizes the skills & resources of other team members
- Asks for help when he/she needs it
- Respects differences & appreciates diversity
- Makes consensus decisions based on what's best for the organization
- Understands & is committed to achieving team goals & objectives
- Trusts, supports, & has genuine concern & regard for all team members
- Strives to orient & support new members
- Recognizes other team member's achievements
- Trains, teaches, & coaches other team members
- Supports the leadership of others
- Does fair share of leadership duties
- Works cooperatively with people outside the team (other teams, shifts, support groups, customers, vendors, suppliers, etc.)
- Takes responsibility
- Is more interested in learning from mistakes than finding someone to blame
- Criticizes the action, not the person
- Keeps promises/commitments
- Does things in a timely manner
- Can admit when he/she is wrong
- Says, "Thank you."
- Says, "I'm sorry."
- Doesn't shoot the messenger
- Problem-solves rather than complains
- Bases opinions/decisions on information not status
- Enjoys being part of the team & takes pride in it

TRAINING ACTIVITY #4:

Self-Assessment: How Do You Rate As A Team Member?

Learning Objective:

To assess your present skills as a team member and make action commitments for continued development.

Directions:

> ## Step One- Individual Exercise
>
> *Rate yourself on a scale of 0–3 on how often you exhibit the following characteristics. Circle the best answer. (5 min.)*
>
> 1. **I understand, support and feel ownership for the team's goals.**
>
> | 0 | 1 | 2 | 3 |
> |---|---|---|---|
> | Never | Sometimes | Most of the Time | Always |
>
> 2. **I am willing to put the team's goals ahead of my own.** (The team member understands that the team's goals and his/her personal goals are ultimately the same. He/she feels a win-win with the team.)
>
> | 0 | 1 | 2 | 3 |
> |---|---|---|---|
> | Never | Sometimes | Most of the Time | Always |
>
> 3. **I listen to everyone on the team.** (The Team Member "actively" listens by trying to understand the other person's point of view before forming an opinion.)
>
> | 0 | 1 | 2 | 3 |
> |---|---|---|---|
> | Never | Sometimes | Most of the Time | Always |
>
> 4. **I am both "task" and "team" focused.** (The team member knows what the goals are and wants to accomplish them, but at the same time is aware of the importance of maintaining and developing the team. Listening to everyone, using conflict constructively, reaching consensus, working for harmony when possible, maintaining good relationships with everyone, compromising when necessary, etc. are all behaviors that make sure the goal/task is accomplished in a manner that does not damage the team.)
>
> | 0 | 1 | 2 | 3 |
> |---|---|---|---|
> | Never | Sometimes | Most of the Time | Always |
>
> 5. **I see conflict as useful and necessary.** (The team member doesn't create conflict for the excitement of it, but also doesn't suppress divergent views. An effective team avoids "group think"—a group phenomenon where people agree to do something no one thinks is a good idea because no one wants to create conflict. This can be avoided by voicing honest opinions and presenting pertinent facts, not just agreeing for the sake of harmony.)
>
> | 0 | 1 | 2 | 3 |
> |---|---|---|---|
> | Never | Sometimes | Most of the Time | Always |

6. **I trust the other members of the team.** (The team member works at getting to know and understand everyone. He/she shares their honest thoughts and feelings to build trust. If he/she senses a lack of trust in a team relationship, a conscious choice is made to do something that begins to change the relationship and not just maintain the status quo.)

0	1	2	3
Never	Sometimes	Most of the Time	Always

7. **I communicate openly and honestly.**

0	1	2	3
Never	Sometimes	Most of the Time	Always

8. **I respect differences and value diversity.** (People are unique; no two are alike. Team members need to spend time understanding one another's similarities, but most especially differences. Stereotyping, judging and false assumptions all get in the way of seeing people as they really are and appreciating their diversity. It would be a dull world if we were all alike. A team needs people with different viewpoints who will think of different ideas, suggestions, innovations, etc.)

0	1	2	3
Never	Sometimes	Most of the Time	Always

9. **I work for consensus.** (Critical to teamwork is the idea that members have a say, everyone listens and out of that process a general agreement is reached. It doesn't mean that each member is in unanimous agreement with the decision, but rather that he/she feels they've been heard, involved, and they will now support and carry-out the Team's decision.)

0	1	2	3
Never	Sometimes	Most of the Time	Always

10. **I utilize the resources of others.** (The team member knows the strengths, knowledge, skills, and abilities of other members and works at tapping those skills for the good of the team. He/she also knows what skills each member is trying to develop and helps them achieve those goals. Periodically, self-directed work teams need to self-correct, that is, look at how the team is helping or hindering members' growth and development and adjust its procedures if it is having a negative impact on people. A team is only as effective as its members.)

0	1	2	3
Never	Sometimes	Most of the Time	Always

Total ☐ (A Perfect Score is 30.)

ACTION COMMITMENTS:

1. Based on your answers to this Self-Assessment, what "Action Commitments" do you want to make at this time to further develop your skills as a team member?

_____

_____

_____

_____

_____

_____

2. Is there some training you feel would improve your skills as a team member?

_____

_____

_____

_____

_____

_____

_____

3. Have every member of the team pair with one other person. In these pairs discuss your answers to the "Self-Assessment/Action Commitments." (Make sure each of you shares "air time" and "actively" listens.)

TRAINING ACTIVITY #5:

The Importance of Team Meetings

■ Team meetings enable teams to: solve problems, schedule work, share new ideas and suggestions, plan for the future and discuss matters relevant to everyone.

■ Team meetings also are the prime way that members experience being a team. These meetings enable team members to get to know one another better, share valuable information, make decisions together, discuss things the team is good at and what it needs to change (self-correct) in order to be more productive, more fun, and personally satisfying to the members.

■ Teams need to meet on a regular basis. Some teams meet daily (for just a few minutes), some weekly, or bi-weekly.

■ Team meetings are also a chance to practice and improve one's listening skills, feedback and disclosure skills.

Keep In Mind:

■ We are social animals and like to get together in teams to feel the community of other people. We need meetings to further enhance our sense of belonging and identification with our team.

■ Meetings are an opportunity to get to know other team members.

■ Meetings are an opportunity to support other's ideas.

■ Meetings are an opportunity to engage in constructive conflict by disagreeing and seeking a better resolution.

■ Meetings enable the team to make decisions together.

■ Meetings enable the team to solve problems and be creative together.

■ Meetings can be fun.

■ Meetings are a time to quickly share information that everyone needs to know.

■ Meetings are a great way to get everyone involved, committed, and responsible for things that need getting done.

■ Size of the meeting: If there are much more than 12 people, it will be difficult to get a lot accomplished (i.e., make consensus decisions). Keep the number limited to all team members plus a few essential guests.

■ A facilitator, team leader or member who acts as team leader, when properly trained, can help the team accomplish its objectives. The facilitator must understand his/her role is to help the team be effective by keeping the team on task, quieting the talkative, drawing out the silent, keeping conflict constructive, keeping the group aware of its process (how it does things), clarifying, moving discussion forward, and reaching resolution. Some teams appoint the same facilitator for all their meetings, and others rotate the role among all the members.

TEAM MEETING ASSESSMENT

Learning Objectives:

To assess team meetings as a way of constantly improving.

Directions:

Step One- Individual Exercise

Answer the following questions about your team's meetings. (10 min.)

Rate your meeting on a scale from 0 (Never) to 4 (Always) by circling your answer.	Never	Seldom	Usually	Most of the Time	Always
1. Everyone understands the purpose of the meeting.	0	1	2	3	4
2. Everyone is involved in the decision-making process.	0	1	2	3	4
3. Everyone is committed to the team's decisions.	0	1	2	3	4
4. Everyone speaks at our meetings. No one person dominates.	0	1	2	3	4
5. The entire team attends.	0	1	2	3	4
6. We have a stated agenda prepared ahead of time with everyone's input.	0	1	2	3	4
7. We carefully plan the order of the agenda, placing the most important items first.	0	1	2	3	4
8. We make sure the meetings are short. (Never more than one hour)	0	1	2	3	4
9. We meet on a regular basis. (daily, weekly, bi-weekly, etc.)	0	1	2	3	4
10. We circulate background information or proposal papers before each meeting (and provide short summaries of very long papers).	0	1	2	3	4
Total:					

(continued)

	Never	Seldom	Usually	Most of the Time	Always
11. We have a meeting facilitator (either the same person or the role shifts among members) to guide the team meeting process.	0	1	2	3	4
12. The facilitator restricts his/her interventions to a minimum (listens more than talks).	0	1	2	3	4
13. We listen to each other.	0	1	2	3	4
14. We paraphrase to make sure we understand what the other person has said.	0	1	2	3	4
15. The facilitator moves the discussion forward when the team gets bogged down or off track.	0	1	2	3	4
16. Everyone understands and accepts resolutions made by the team.	0	1	2	3	4
17. Team members are given feedback when they delay or divert the team's progress in discussion, problem-solving, etc.	0	1	2	3	4
18. The team is able to reach consensus in decision-making.	0	1	2	3	4
19. The team is able to resolve issues.	0	1	2	3	4
20. Team members seek clarification if they need it.	0	1	2	3	4
21. The atmosphere in the meeting is relaxed, comfortable and informal.	0	1	2	3	4
Total:					

(*continued*)

	Never	Seldom	Usually	Most of the Time	Always
22. Discussion is closed when it's clear a resolution has been reached.	0	1	2	3	4
23. Decisions are not postponed simply because they're difficult.	0	1	2	3	4
24. Before the end of the meeting the facilitator gives:					
• A brief clear summary of what has been agreed on	0	1	2	3	4
• Members are asked to confirm the actions they've committed to	0	1	2	3	4
• A time and place are set for the next meeting	0	1	2	3	4
25. Minutes of the meeting are recorded and distributed to members, leaders, support people, etc.	0	1	2	3	4
Total					
Total of All Columns					
Grand Total					

(A Perfect Score is 108.)

Step Two: Team Exercise

When everyone has finished the "Team Meeting Assessment," discuss your answers with the entire team and then answer the following questions together: (20 min.)

■ What do we see as the strengths of our team meetings?

_____

_____

_____

_____

■ What are some areas we need to improve?

_____

_____

_____

_____

■ Discuss and agree on the *actions* we feel need to be taken to make our team meetings more effective.

_____

_____

_____

_____

ACTIONS TO FACILITATE "POSITIVE" GROUP DYNAMICS

A team meeting facilitator can be helpful by doing the following:

1. Paying attention to what is said and not said, the mood of the group, the energy level, body language
2. Constantly thinking: What does this group need in order to be more effective?
3. Role modeling "active" listening (paraphrasing, speaking less than listening, listening for feelings, etc.)
4. Helping people get to know each other and building trust
5. Making sure the atmosphere is relaxed, comfortable, and free of fear
6. Making sure everyone participates
7. Keeping the group focused and on track by making them aware of the times when they get off task and guiding them back
8. Encouraging open and honest expression of ideas
9. Not suppressing conflict, but insisting the team focus on the problem, not the personalities
10. Providing structure for the group (i.e., an agenda, goals, objectives)
11. Sharing leadership so the team is not dependent on one person
12. Helping individuals balance their personal needs with the team's needs
13. Providing the group with feedback to recognize its achievements and correct its problems
14. Helping the group set ground rules, make effective decisions, form goals, and measure/assess itself
15. Focusing on the process: How information is gathered, how decisions are made, how problems are solved or delayed
16. Designing the physical layout of the meeting room so people feel comfortable, relaxed, able to see each other, and all feel equal
17. Making sure the organization supports the team
18. Coaching/counseling team members
19. Knowing when and when *not* to intervene
20. Teaching/training the team members in understanding group dynamics

TRAINING ACTIVITY #5:

Developing Active Listening Skills

WHY LISTENING IS THE #1 SKILL OF AN EFFECTIVE TEAM MEMBER/TEAM LEADER

If you think your listening could use some improvement, you have a lot of company—most people are poor listeners. This has been borne out by standardized tests that found people only hear about 25% of the message and by the intangible evidence all around us that good listeners are rare indeed.

We think listening is the single most important communication skill a team member or leader must possess. If you want proof of this, think for a moment of the last time someone really listened to you. It may have been recently or a while ago. Try to remember how you felt.

Most people say they felt some or all of the following:

- they mattered as a person
- they were important
- they were worth the time spent on listening to them
- they had valuable ideas, resources
- they felt empowered

Learning Objective:

To assess present level of listening skills and develop skills further.

Step One- Individual Exercise

Think of the "best listener" you know. What does he/she do? (5 min.)
List answers here:

_____   _____

_____   _____

_____   _____

_____   _____

_____   _____

Step Two- Individual Exercise

Compare your list with the one on the next page. (5 min.)

"ACTIVE" LISTENING

Psychologist Carl Rogers called what good listeners do—ACTIVE LISTENING—because it's not a passive activity. As you can see from the following list, good listeners do many things.

WHAT DOES A GOOD LISTENER DO?

- Gives eye contact
- Indicates they're paying attention (i.e., leans forward, nods)
- Concentrates on the listener—is "other person" focused
- Stops thinking about anything else
- Doesn't mentally rehearse what they're going to say next while the speaker is talking
- Doesn't interrupt
- Doesn't complete the speaker's sentences (assuming they already know what is going to be said)
- Doesn't ask questions that redirect the conversation
- Stays focused on what the speaker said
- Paraphrases (Restates what they heard the speaker say, not word-for-word because that would be just parroting. Instead, the active listener checks to make sure what they heard is really what the speaker said/ meant. For example: "Let me see if I understand what you just said. You think the meeting we had yesterday was a waste of time because . . . Is that right?"
- Observes body language; posture, position of hands & legs, eyes, gestures, space, territory, seating
- Listens for content (i.e., words, information, details) and feelings (i.e., tone of voice, eyes gestures, expressions, silence, emotions)
- Listens "between-the-lines" for intentions: incongruence between words & behavior, omissions, energy level, commitment to act
- Respects the speaker & doesn't judge
- Keeps an open mind
- Understands that the purpose of "active" listening is to understand the speaker and not necessarily agree with him/her
- Refrains from solving the other person's problem, instead helps him/ her talk through the problem and find their own solution (That is much more esteem building than having someone tell you what they would do and what you "should" do.)
- Accepts whatever the speaker has to say as their opinion which they're entitled to express without punishment
- Makes sure they're ready to listen: tunes out or eliminates distractions or, if that's not possible, asks to meet at a later time
- Most of all, good listeners value listening and believe it's important. That's why they make time to do it!

LISTENING SELF-ASSESSMENT

Indicate with a check (✔) how you feel you are presently doing in each skill area. Choose one.

Skill Areas:	Having Difficulty	Doing Alright But Need Developing	Skill I'm Good At
Listening for Facts			
Listening for Feelings			
Paraphrasing			
Expressing My Feelings			
Asking Open-ended Questions			
Being Open-minded			
Not Interrupting			
Willing to Confront Conflict			
Remembering Information			
Not Completing Other's Sentences			
Not Giving Advice			
Making Eye Contact			
Observing Body Language			
Comfortable with Silence			
Other-Person Focused			
Taking Notes for Retention			
Not Getting Defensive			
Establishing Trust			
Encouraging Feedback			
Not Evaluating or Judging			
Not Mentally Rehearsing Next Statement			

WHY EFFECTIVE LISTENING IS "GOOD" BUSINESS

- The listening organization is the one most likely to pick-up quickly on changes in the environment (customers, markets, etc.)
- Good listeners reduce the distortion of information flowing up, down, and across.
- Listening to people is empowering in the sense that it builds self-esteem and confidence.
- The best way to gain commitment from people is to listen to what they have to say and act on what you hear.
- Listening reduces/eliminates the wasted efforts resulting from miscommunication.
- Listening promotes risk-taking by encouraging people to speak-up, try new ideas, innovate.
- Listening underscores the belief that others have valuable information, expertise, and ideas.
- Listening for understanding eliminates or reduces many of the causes of conflict.
- Without listening, participation is impossible.
- Without listening, learning is impossible.
- Effective listening saves time, which saves money.
- Team synergy is the product of good listening.
- Great ideas don't have a chance of being implemented unless someone in the organization is willing to listen.
- Customer service is first and foremost good listening.
- Listening is the best way to stay in touch.
- Teams rely on consensus decision-making which is impossible without effective listening.
- Listening is the number one job of leadership. Coaching, counseling, and inspiring are not possible without active listening.

THE IMPORTANCE OF LISTENING
TO LEADING/FACILITATING A TEAM

Effective leaders/facilitators listen to individuals and to the team as a whole. They constantly pay attention to what is happening and ask themselves:

■ Where is this group in terms of its development? (Are people still getting to know each other, building trust, etc?)
■ What is the energy level of the group right now? (high? low?)
■ What feelings (conscious and unconscious) are being expressed today? (frustration? anger?)
■ What does this team need? (more fun? some success? questions answered? more structure? more agreement? more conflict? a "clearing-of-the-air" session? problem-solving?)

Effective leaders/facilitators know that listening to people increases their self-esteem and, therefore, they are more likely to:

■ offer suggestions
■ problem-solve
■ take risks/innovate
■ speak openly & honestly
■ get involved
■ bring problems to light
■ discuss their honest feelings
■ be creative
■ learn

All of these actions are key to bringing about the kind of employee involvement high-performing teams are all about.

TRAINING ACTIVITY #7

Developing Coaching Skills

Learning Objective:

To understand the qualities and skills involved in effective coaching.

Directions:

Step One- Team Exercise

Conduct a "brainstorming"* session on: "the qualities of good coaches" (Choose a facilitator to write down the qualities on a flip chart as team members call them out.)

Write the final list here:

_____	_____
_____	_____
_____	_____
_____	_____
_____	_____
_____	_____
_____	_____
_____	_____

*See "*Guidelines for Brainstorming*" on page 27.

Step Two- Team Exercise

Conduct a discussion comparing your list with the one below:

Qualities of Good Coaches

A good coach is someone who-

- believes in you
- sees potential in you that no one else (no even you) sees
- provides encouragement
- has faith
- has patience
- develops your skills
- is a good listener
- gives honest, sincere feedback (positive & negative)
- communicates openly & honestly
- always takes feelings into consideration
- is a good role model
- challenges you to do your best (and won't settle for less)
- teaches skills & attitudes
- fosters independence (teaches you "how to fish" instead of giving you a fish)
- let's you make your own decisions
- won't give-up (and won't let you give-up)
- is empathic & understanding
- is firm but fair
- focuses on results
- keeps you on target
- provides support & guidance
- provides the necessary tools
- let's you solve the problem
- removes barriers
- keeps promises
- focuses on goals
- handles pressure
- focuses on strengths

- works hard
- gives credit to others
- is accessible
- focuses on learning from mistakes rather than placing blame
- builds teamwork
- fosters cooperation
- doesn't abuse their authority
- focuses on the future (not the past)
- inspires
- celebrates successes
- respects & values diversity
- helps everyone develop his/her personal style
- sets high expectations & helps you attain them
- has a good sense of humor
- is enthusiastic
- is "other person" focused
- has the courage to stick-up for what's right
- is interested in what's best for the enterprise (not self-interested)
- can handle a crisis
- gets everyone involved; demands 100% participation
- puts learning above winning
- is optimistic
- values human beings
- is a change agent
- is flexible
- doesn't hold a grudge
- likes what they're doing
- empowers others
- has self-esteem

CONDUCTING AN EFFECTIVE COACHING SESSION:

- Make sure the atmosphere is conducive to good listening and dialog. (i.e., a quiet, private room with comfortable chairs facing each other, and no outside distractions).
- Put other person at ease.
- Clarify the reason for the discussion. Make sure you're both in agreement about why you're there and what you want to accomplish.
- Ask open-ended questions that invite the other person to state the problem or concern from their point of view. (i.e., "What do you think about. . ?").
- Practice active listening by observing, concentrating, and stopping at various times to paraphrase in order to make sure you understand what's being said thus far.
- Observe the other person's body language (i.e., posture, facial expressions).
- Paraphrase feelings and intent, not just words.
- Ask questions that remain focused on what speaker has said.
- Stop at various points to summarize the discussion.
- Give feedback when asked.
- Find out what type of coaching the person is asking for: technical skill development, interpersonal skill development, etc.
- Offer suggestions when appropriate.
- Mutually agree on next step and next meeting.
- Decide on what each of you is committed to doing for the next session.
- Close the session by each summarizing thoughts and feelings on the session.
- After the session write notes and process what happened. Think about:

  - What do you know about the person?

  - What don't you know?

  - How could you observe them with others prior to the next session?

  - What strengths do they have?

  - What skills do they want to develop?

  - What are they having difficulty with?

  - Any other pertinent information?

  - What are your thoughts and feelings concerning the session just concluded?

  - Anything you want to remember to do/ask next session?

NOTES:

NOTES:

ACTION TEN

Changing Organizational Systems

- *Measuring & Evaluating Teams*
  - *High-Involvement Exercise*

- *Peer Assessments*
  - *Sample Performance Review*

- *Career Development: What do you do when there is no ladder to climb?*

The Importance of Reward Systems
  - *Incentive Compensation Systems That Work*
  - *What is Needed to Make Incentive Plans Effective*
  - *Companies Using Incentive Systems*
  - *Rewards & Motivation*
  - *High-Involvement Exercise*

Traditional organizations have systems for measurement, assessment, reward, and career development that all focus on *individual* achievement. These systems become major barriers because they conflict with developing and supporting teams. Therefore, how we measure, appraise, promote, and reward must be rethought and redesigned.

In **"Action Ten"** we're going to focus on:

- Changing what & how we measure
- Changing how we currently appraise
- Changing career development: What do you do when there is no ladder to climb?
- Changing how we reward

MEASURING & EVALUATING TEAMS

High-performing teams need feedback on how they're doing so they can "self-correct" and improve their processes. How to measure and evaluate, therefore, is very important. There is no *one* best way. Each organization is unique and needs to involve its people in defining a measurement and evaluation system that works for them. Typically, companies have not been very effective in this area.

In 1991 a survey conducted by the American Productivity & Quality Center found that almost 40 percent of the 417 people surveyed said their performance was not evaluated in a fair manner.

Successful organizations address this problem by involving people in designing systems that provide accurate feedback. **The best measurement systems include the following features:**

- Focusing on what's important to a customer (both internal and external). If you don't know, find out and use a variety of methods (face-to-face questionnaires, 800 numbers, etc.)
- Measuring the team's performance by gathering feedback on things like:
  - Production (yield, number of customer complaints, etc.)
  - Maintaining the technical system (machines, maintenance, etc.)
  - Response time
  - Customer service (i.e., how fast phones are answered)
  - Safety
  - Waste/scrap
  - Relations with suppliers/vendors
  - Overtime
  - Costs
- Team measurements based on team goals that align with department/division/company goals

■ Reward and compensation systems tied to measurement and evaluation.

■ Teams set individual performance standards for team members based on their:
- Knowledge of multiple jobs
- Accuracy
- Completion of work
- Attendance
- Problem-solving
- Continuous improvement
- Learning & development
- Cooperation, helpfulness, participation, relationships with others, commitment, responsibility, etc.
- Technical proficiency
- Attendance at meetings & level of involvement
- Time management
- Leadership skills
- Interpersonal skills (communication, listening, conflict management, etc.)

A good measurement system continually changes in response to changing conditions.

HIGH-INVOLVEMENT EXERCISE

Learning Objective:

To think through and discuss how your team is measured.

Directions:

Step One- Individual Exercise

Answer each question as an individual. (5 min.)

1. How does your team currently get feedback?

_____

_____

_____

_____

_____

2. What does your team currently measure?

_____

_____

_____

_____

3. Are there other dimensions the team should be measuring (i.e., teamwork, customer service, etc.)?

_____

_____

_____

_____

_____

Step Two- Team Exercise

Discuss your individual answers with the entire team and reach consensus* on Question #3. (25 min.)
*See "*Guidelines for Reaching Consensus*" on page 7.

_____

_____

_____

_____

_____

_____

_____

_____

_____

_____

_____

_____

_____

_____

PEER ASSESSMENTS

Team members do not usually assess one another until they've been together for a period of time, when they do assess, certain assumptions are made about the benefits of peer assessment over traditional forms of appraisal:

- Peers know one another better than an appraiser outside the team.
- Peers can see how someone works (both technically and as a team member).
- Peers provide several raters, not just one opinion, therefore, a fairer assessment is possible.
- Peers have most to gain or lose by providing fair, accurate feedback.
- Peer pressure is a powerful motivator.
- Peers know each other's strengths and areas to develop.

We are seeing more peer assessment as more and more companies move to team-based cultures. Some companies have been doing this for quite awhile and we need to learn from their experiences.

COMPANIES USING PEER REVIEW*

GORE & ASSOCIATES has used peer reviews since the company was started in 1958. Every employee is ranked on the basis of his/her contribution to the company goals and paid accordingly. The ranking is done by a compensation committee at each Gore facility (about 40 plants each with no more than 200 people) made up of 6–10 workers, with input from peers and customers. These "contribution lists," as they're called, are compiled several times a year.

QUAKER OATS PET FOODS' entire performance appraisal process is made up of peer review. SDWTs make all compensation and promotion decisions on this basis. Peers evaluate how well each person is doing in terms of the work processes and, equally important, how effective they are as a team member (spirit, communication, problem-solving, etc.). They use a pay-for-knowledge compensation system that rewards people for learning new skills.

*As reported in "An Early Review of Peer Review," *Training Magazine,* July 1991.

PERFORMANCE REVIEW

In high-performance organizations people need feedback on how they're doing. Measurement provides feedback on production/service, but team members and leaders also need feedback on their development. The best assessments are custom designed by each organization, but we have created a "generic" version that can be adapted for any organization.

The following "Performance Review" was created for team members. Usually each team member fills this out on themselves and on one another. These forms are then submitted to the Team Leader* who then conducts a one-on-one session with each team member. The discussion focuses on:

• How the team member assessed themselves
• How the team member's peers assessed him/her (typically the team's average scores are revealed not each individual's rating)

• How the Team Leader rated the team member
• What strengths were indicated
• What areas received low scores

The session ends with a plan for providing the training/coaching needed by the individual for further learning and development.

A mature team (two or more years old) which has developed high levels of trust might not need to involve a Team Leader and could discuss these ratings openly. Going through the Team Leader could be a transition step to enable the team to get feedback in a "safe" way until they're ready to handle it more directly.

Many organizations are also using 360° feedback appraisals for team leaders and team members. This method involves feedback from peers, leaders, support functions, internal & external customers, etc. and gives people important feedback on how effective they are from several points of view.

---

*The term, "Team Leader," as we're using it here means the leader outside the team (not any member of the team). Some organizations call this person a supervisor, manager, coach, etc.

PERFORMANCE REVIEW

Directions: Complete the following form by rating from 1 (to a low degree) to 10 (to a high degree) the extent to which the person being reviewed demonstrates skills/competencies in these areas. Under "Explanation" explain your rating.

Date _____

Name of Reviewer: _____
Name of Person Being Reviewed: Self? Other? _____

TECHNICAL SKILLS:

Low   High

1. Computer competency   1 2 3 4 5 6 7 8 9 10

    Explanation: _____

2. Time management   1 2 3 4 5 6 7 8 9 10

    Explanation: _____

3. Order processing   1 2 3 4 5 6 7 8 9 10

    Explanation: _____

4. Telephone skills   1 2 3 4 5 6 7 8 9 10

    Explanation: _____

5. Record keeping   1 2 3 4 5 6 7 8 9 10

    Explanation: _____

WORK HABITS:

Low   High

1. Attendance   1 2 3 4 5 6 7 8 9 10

    Explanation: _____

2. Accuracy   1 2 3 4 5 6 7 8 9 10

    Explanation: _____

3. Timeliness   1 2 3 4 5 6 7 8 9 10

    Explanation: _____

4. Initiative   1 2 3 4 5 6 7 8 9 10

    Explanation: _____

5. Commitment   1 2 3 4 5 6 7 8 9 10

    Explanation: _____

6. Organization   1 2 3 4 5 6 7 8 9 10

    Explanation: _____

7. Productivity   1 2 3 4 5 6 7 8 9 10

    Explanation: _____

8. Responsibility   1 2 3 4 5 6 7 8 9 10

    Explanation: _____

INTERPERSONAL/TEAM SKILLS:

                                    Low   High

1. Works well with others   1 2 3 4 5 6 7 8 9 10

    Explanation: _____

2. Communication (oral)   1 2 3 4 5 6 7 8 9 10

    Explanation: _____

3. Communication (written)   1 2 3 4 5 6 7 8 9 10

    Explanation: _____

4. Listening   1 2 3 4 5 6 7 8 9 10

    Explanation: _____

5. Helps other team members   1 2 3 4 5 6 7 8 9 10

    Explanation: _____

6. Demonstrates leadership   1 2 3 4 5 6 7 8 9 10

    Explanation: _____

7. Trains & coaches others   1 2 3 4 5 6 7 8 9 10

    Explanation: _____

8. Contributes suggestions,   1 2 3 4 5 6 7 8 9 10
    ideas for improvements, etc.
    Explanation: _____

9. Problem-solving   1 2 3 4 5 6 7 8 9 10

    Explanation: _____

10. Decision-making

         1 2 3 4 5 6 7 8 9 10

         Explanation: _____

11. Conflict management

         1 2 3 4 5 6 7 8 9 10

         Explanation: _____

QUALITY/CUSTOMER SERVICE SKILLS:

Low   High

1. Customer-driven

         1 2 3 4 5 6 7 8 9 10

         Explanation: _____

2. Demonstrates commitment to quality

         1 2 3 4 5 6 7 8 9 10

         Explanation: _____

3. Performs quality checks

         1 2 3 4 5 6 7 8 9 10

         Explanation: _____

4. Works cost-effectively

         1 2 3 4 5 6 7 8 9 10

         Explanation: _____

PERSONAL DEVELOPMENT:

Low   High

1. Demonstrates life-long learning

         1 2 3 4 5 6 7 8 9 10

         Explanation: _____

2. Enrolled in classes/training

         1 2 3 4 5 6 7 8 9 10

         Explanation: _____

3. Improves quality, customer-service, cost, etc.

         1 2 3 4 5 6 7 8 9 10

         Explanation: _____

4. Seeks new & better ways to do things

         1 2 3 4 5 6 7 8 9 10

         Explanation: _____

5. Seeks out information on business

         1 2 3 4 5 6 7 8 9 10

         Explanation: _____

SAFETY HABITS:												

                                                             Low   High

1. Understands & practices safety procedures   1 2 3 4 5 6 7 8 9 10

            Explanation: _____

2. Practices good housekeeping   1 2 3 4 5 6 7 8 9 10

            Explanation: _____

3. Works safely with others   1 2 3 4 5 6 7 8 9 10

            Explanation: _____

4. Shows concern for others safety   1 2 3 4 5 6 7 8 9 10

            Explanation: _____

5. Knows what to do in an emergency   1 2 3 4 5 6 7 8 9 10

            Explanation: _____

FOLLOW-UP TRAINING/COACHING PLANNED:

Description:	**Date Scheduled:**
_____	_____
_____	_____
_____	_____
_____	_____
_____	_____
_____	_____
_____	_____
_____	_____

CAREER DEVELOPMENT:

What do you do when there is no ladder to climb?

As organizations become flatter, traditional promotion and career development opportunities decrease, creating a very serious dilemma: At a time when we need highly-motivated, committed people, we have fewer ways to reward high-performers. There is no one answer to this problem, but successful organizations are doing some or all of the following things:

- Creating "career bands" instead of levels that reward people for in-depth knowledge and skills in a technical area. (They can advance without being forced to go into management in order to make more money.)
- Horizontal movement of people, so they can acquire new knowledge and skills in a variety of departments/divisions/business units
- Promoting people to new positions created through work redesign
- Increasing team leaders, trainers, facilitators, coaches, etc. that support teams
- Providing people with multiple skills (and, sometimes, paying them more money for each skill in which the team certifies they're proficient)
- Training as a way of growing and developing by constantly learning, and improving
- Redesigning reward systems to create a pay-for-performance system whereby the "smarter" an individual or a team works, the more money they earn. The most popular methods are: gainsharing, profit-sharing, pay-for-skills, pay-for-knowledge, and lump-sum bonuses. Companies like GE and Monsanto are experimenting with a variety of different reward systems that all aim to link pay with performance. They recognize that reward systems are extremely important when there is no ladder to climb.
- High-performing teams can give team members many of the motivators the traditional system lacked:
  —more money for high-performance
  —more authority & control
  —more opportunities to contribute ideas, suggestions, etc.
  —leadership opportunities
  —fulfillment of social needs which teamwork satisfies
  —learning, training, growth & development
  —more marketable skills
  —more decision-making power
  —more involvement & participation
  —more status
  —more influence

THE IMPORTANCE OF REWARD SYSTEMS

> A survey by the Public Agenda Foundation interviewed 845 blue and white collar workers and found that 45% believed there was no link between their performance and their pay.

As organizations become flatter, they remove many of the traditional opportunities for career advancement. Changing the reward system becomes very important as a way to reward high-performance without necessarily being promoted vertically.

When organizations are redesigned, they can achieve their greatest gains by examining and changing the way they reward individuals and teams. High-performance adds variety, challenge, and many other "motivators" to work, but people working "smarter" also want to be financially rewarded. It's a genuine "win-win" when the company and the people share profits/gains. Executive bonuses have traditionally been a way to provide incentives for exceptional results. In the high-performance workplace *all* workers can potentially be rewarded for what they accomplish as individuals and as teams.

Incentive pay is spreading into manufacturing and service industries according to a recent article in Fortune Magazine ("Here Come Richer, Riskier Pay Plans," Dec. 1988). Gain-sharing, profit-sharing, lump-sum bonuses, pay-for-skills, and pay-for-knowledge are the most common types and all attempt to link pay with performance instead of just time on the job. The challenge is to design an effective pay system that really motivates people and rewards them for improving the bottom line and forwarding the strategic plan. According to many experts, most incentive compensation plans don't work because of poor design (i.e., quantity rewarded, but quality suffers) or poor administration (employees don't understand how it works and, therefore, don't know how what they do makes a difference).

> The American Productivity & Quality Center reports 75% of employers in 1988 used at least one form of nontraditional pay.

WHAT IS NEEDED TO MAKE INCENTIVE PLANS EFFECTIVE:

- A clear business strategy that ties incentives to the company goals
- Involve employees in designing a customized system that fits the uniqueness of your organization
- Management must be willing to listen, act on ideas, and share information
- Focus on what can be measured. benchmark performance, and track results

- Separate incentives from base pay to emphasize the link between the employee's performance and rewards
- Make sure employees understand the plan and know what they need to do to make a difference.
- Some of the most successful plans combine the best features of many different types of reward systems.
- Be flexible and change the system as conditions change

INCENTIVE COMPENSATION SYSTEMS THAT WORK:

PROFIT-SHARING: This is the most widely used compensation incentive (more than 30% of US companies). Employees receive an annual bonus which varies depending on the company's profits for that time period. It pays only if the company has profits deemed sufficient to pay-out. It is simple to administer and easy and understand. However, annual payments seem too long to adequately motivate and often employees feel that what they do doesn't have as much impact on the profits as key decisions made by other people (top executives, customers, etc.).

GAINSHARING: Many experts think this is the best incentive system for motivating people. If a unit of an organization (plant, division, department, etc.) surpasses a predetermined goal, all members share in a bonus. This rewards employees for results (producing a product, delivering a service, etc.), they can influence, measure, track, and improve. Gainsharing also encourages teamwork, trust, and employee involvement.

LUMP-SUM BONUSES: Employees receive a one time cash payment. This holds down wage and salary increases, thus controlling fixed costs. In order for this to work, employees must trust management or they might feel the pay outs are subjective and unfair.

PAY-FOR-SKILLS, PAY-FOR-KNOWLEDGE: Under this plan, an employee's salary or wage increases each time he/she masters a task or skill block. Mastery needs to be defined and then tested. When a company's strategic plan involves people becoming multi-skilled and learning new jobs, job consolidation, or continuous improvement, this form of incentive can be very effective. In order to make this work required skills need to be identified and assigned a pay grade. Needs assessment and training also play a critical role. When done successfully, employees become multi-skilled, the company gains more flexibility, and everyone wins. The training costs are substantial, but the increased skill levels of people, the effectiveness of teams, and the ability of everyone to solve problems increases.

COMPANIES USING INCENTIVE SYSTEMS

We are seeing an increase in incentive programs with 26% of U.S. companies using some form of gainsharing.

- **Corning, Inc.** announced that eventually all their plants will have a gainsharing program where all employees will benefit from the productivity of their plant.
- At **Carrier Corp.** employees participate in "Improshare." When workers produce more acceptable quality goods compared to their benchmark, the resulting savings in labor costs are split 50-50 between the company and the employees (everybody from maintenance workers to machinists to managers gets the same percentage bonus). The result has been increased teamwork, 24% higher productivity, and a lower reject rate.
- At **Lincoln Electric** there is no hourly rate. Workers get a piecework rate and yearly merit ratings based on their dependability, ideas, quality, and output. Based on these ratings, employees receive year-end bonuses that average 97.6% of their regular earnings. Lincoln Electric has had impressive results: 54 years without a losing quarter and 40 years without layoffs.

- **Nucor Steel's** plan uses profit sharing on top of small group incentives. Factory workers at 5 steel mills earn weekly bonuses based on the number of tons of acceptable quality steel they produce. Productive teams average well over 100% of their base pay. Base wages are kept low, but total earnings are higher than the industry average. Workers who are late lose their bonus for the day and workers who are more than 30 minutes late lose their bonus for the week. Manager's salaries are also based on plant productivity; they receive bonuses based on return on plant assets. Plant managers receive bonuses based on overall return on equity. At times managers can suffer even though workers continue to earn bonuses based on output. At the end of the year, Nucor distributes 10% of pretax earnings to all employees. The results: In 1987 Nucor turned out more than twice as much steel as its larger competitors. Ken Iverson, the CEO, credits much of this to Nucor's incentive plan which makes each crew want to make more money than the previous shift so production rises all day long. They haven't had a losing quarter since '65 and no layoffs for over 20 years.

REWARDS & HUMAN MOTIVATION

Money, although very important, is just one of the reasons we work (and for most of us, not the most important reason). Below is a list of motivators that high-performance workplaces provide:

> A sense of **ACHIEVEMENT**
> **RECOGNITION**
> the **WORK ITSELF** (redesigned work should
> have variety, wholeness, ect. built into it)
> **RESPONSIBILITY**
> **AUTONOMY** (control)
> **AUTHORITY** (empowerment)
> **GROWTH & LEARNING**
> **LEADERSHIP**
> **RELATIONSHIPS**
> **STATUS**
> **COMPANY POLICY & ADM.**
> **COMPENSATION**
> **BENEFITS**
> **WORKING CONDITIONS** (safe, comfortable, ect.)
> **SECURITY** (being multi-skilled increases one's
> sense of job security)

Motivation is the energy that helps us satisfy our basic, social, and higher level needs. We all know what motivation looks like at work: People who are responsible, committed, and striving to do their best. A motivated workforce can accomplish almost anything. High-performance is all about achieving competitive advantage through a motivated workforce.

Why is high-performance more motivating?

It helps us satisfy more of our needs. Traditional work focused almost exclusively on BASIC needs, providing workers with security, benefits, and salary. High-performance models add many other motivators: Constantly learning new skills satisfies our basic needs by making us more marketable. Teamwork also satisfies important SOCIAL needs that traditional work tried (unsuccessfully) to block. And redesigning work so that everyone has a "good" job with variety, challenge, growth, and learning, satisfies higher level SELF-ACTUALIZING needs to be the best we can be. All of us want a sense of achievement in our work and high-performance work cultures give us opportunities to use *all* our skills and talents. Human beings have *unlimited* potential as long as we keep learning.

HIGH-INVOLVEMENT EXERCISE

Examining & Redesigning the Organization's Systems

Learning Objective:

To begin to examine and redesign the organization's systems.

Directions:

Step One- Individual Exercise

As an individual answer the following questions: (10 min.)

1. How effective is our current measurement system?

_____

_____

•   How could it be made more effective?

_____

_____

2. How effective is our current appraisal system?

_____

_____

•   How could it be made more effective?

_____

_____

3. How effective is our organization's career development?

_____

_____

• How could it be made more effective?

_____

_____

4. How effective is our current reward system?

_____

_____

• How could it be made more effective?

_____

_____

Step Two- Team Exercise

Discuss your answers with the entire team. (30 min.)

_____

_____

_____

_____

_____

_____

_____

_____

_____

_____

NOTES:

ACTION ELEVEN

Building-In Continuous Learning & Improvement

- *Process Vs. "Program"*
- *Case Studies of Continuous Learning & High-Performance:*
  - *Johnsonville Foods, Inc.*
  - *Quaker Oats Pet Food*
- *Bibliography*
- *Videos*
- *Training*

Process	Vs.	Program
Permanent—Long term change		A Quick Fix
Everyone Involved		Management Dictated
Results Evolve Over Time		Immediate Results Expected
Everyone Continually Trained		Very Little Training
Leaders Involved		Leaders Delegate
Dialogues, Small Group Sessions, etc. (Build Commitment Through Participation & Involvement)		Speeches, Slogans, etc. ("Selling")
Organization Redesigned With Work Teams As Basic Building Block		Temporary Teams Formed, But Organization Still Hierarchical
Total Cultural Change		Limited Scope of Change
Seen As Long Term Investment		Seen As Short Term Experiment
On-Going, Continual Learning Process That Has No End		Ends Whenever Management Wants It To End

PROCESS VS. PROGRAM

When American managers think of change, too often they think in terms of implementing a "program." Quality Circles were programs and, for the most part, they didn't last. What's needed is an on-going change process that completely transforms the organization.

Most American workers can tell you about "programs" that came and went and resulted in a lot of cynicism. What is needed is a process by which the total organization changes. Instituting teams in a hierarchical, traditional structure is not enough. A great team at the bottom of the organization is too limited in its scope; it can't do much to satisfy a customer unless the entire or-

ganization is geared to empower and support.

Transforming our traditional organizations into high-performance models involves recreating almost everything: attitudes, skills, systems, structures, and leadership.

One of the greatest challenges facing high-performance organizations is to never reach an end state. We need to create an organization that is constantly learning and changing. Each organization must develop its own unique way of renewing itself. We'd like to give you two examples of companies that have done this for 10 and 20 years, respectively.

Case Study #1: A Company That Never Stops Learning

Johnsonville Foods, Inc.
Sheboygan, Wisconsin

- Change started in 1980 by CEO, Ralph Stayer
- Line workers select and train new hires and assume most of the traditional personnel functions
- Annual across-the-board raises eliminated in favor of a pay-for-responsibility system (as people take on new duties—budgeting, training, etc.—they earn additional base income)
  In addition, a company performance share, gives each employee a fixed percentage of pretax profits every six months (individual performance shares linked to appraisal system designed and administered by line production workers)
- Hierarchical layers went from six to three
- Self-directed work teams make all decisions about scheduling, performance standards, assignments, budgets, quality measures, and capital improvements.
- Operations teams assumed all the supervisor's functions and there are no longer supervisors (former supervisors assumed other jobs and some moved into technical positions)
- Quality control no longer checks quality—workers do that themselves. Now it provides technical support to production people.
- The personnel department disappeared and was replaced by a learning and personnel development team that helps individual employees develop their goals and figure out how Johnsonville can help them reach these.
- Each employee gets an educational allowance to use for their own learning, growth, & development
- 65% of all employees are involved in some type of formal education
- Stayer's vision for Johnsonville: "A company that never stops learning"
- Johnsonville Foods as a company believes that helping people fulfill their potential is a moral responsibility and good business because learning, growing people are good workers. They have initiative, creativity, and this benefits the companies they work for. Ralph Stayer believes "people want to be great."
- Learning is change at Johnsonville
- Achieving better performance means a permanent change in the way you think and run a business. "Change of this kind is not a single transaction but a journey. . ."
- Change is the real job of every effective business leader
- Success can be the greatest enemy because it causes complacency. To combat this teams at Johnsonville are redesigning their systems and structures to continue to respond to customers, market conditions, etc.

[As reported in "How I Learned to Let My Workers Lead," by Ralph Stayer, Harvard Business Review (Nov.–Dec. 1990)]

Case Study #2: Twenty Years of Teamwork—And Still Going

Quaker Oats Pet Food
Topeka, Kansas

- Started in 1971 as an experiment for America in socio-technical systems
- A start-up facility designed around the concept of self-regulating work teams
- Greatest year-to-year productivity increase of all the plants in the corporation (previous owner, General Foods)
- One of the world's most productive factories
- Entire plant made-up of teams (on plant floor and in office)
- Everyone rotates jobs
- To be at "plant rate" one must be able to do all jobs (a pay-for-skills reward system)
- After twenty years, everyone is at plant rate, a gainsharing reward system is now being instituted
- Three times as many people are now employed as when they started (about three-hundred employees), but no layers have been added to the original three

- Job stability is stressed (never had layoffs); management highly committed to work force
- During low production periods, workers do other jobs, such as plant maintenance
- Two teams on each shift do the whole job (quality control, maintenance, sanitation, processing, and warehousing)
- Rules and regulations are kept to a minimum to allow maximum flexibility
- Teams hire new members
- Teams manage the entire work processes from start to finish
- Keeping up with technological changes is an on-going continuous learning process
- Change seen as a constant (i.e., for twentieth anniversary, a conference was held for all employees to explore how to renew the system)
- After twenty years of success, the journey is never over and customer satisfaction is still a moving target

(As reported in video, "*Topeka Pride: 20 Years of Teamwork.*" Blue Sky Productions, (1991)

BIBLIOGRAPHY

Bluestone, Barry & Irving. *Negotiating the Future.* New York: Basic Books, 1992.

Byham, William C. *Zapp! The Lightning of Empowerment.* New York: Harmony Books, 1990.

Goodman, Paul S. *Designing Effective Workgroups.* San Francisco: Jossey-Bass, 1986.

Hackman, J.R. & G.R. Oldham. *Work Redesign.* Reading, MA: Addisson-Wesley, 1980.

*Harper, Ann & Bob. *Self-Directed Work Teams & Your Organization: Two Assessment Tools.* New York: MW Corporation, 1991.

*Harper, Ann & Bob. *Skill-Building for Self-Directed Team Members: A Complete Course.* New York: MW Corporation, 1992.

*Harper, Ann & Bob. *Succeeding As A Self-Directed Work Team: 20 Important Questions Answered.* New York: MW Corporation, 1990.

Ketchum, Lyman D. & Eric Trist. *All Teams Are Not Created Equal: How Employee Empowerment "Really" Works.* Newbury Park: Sage Publications, 1992.

Lawler, E. E. *High Involvement Management.* San Francisco: Jossey-Bass, Inc., 1986.

Lawler, E. E. *Strategic Pay: Aligning Organizational Strategies and Pay Systems.* San Francisco: Jossey-Bass, Inc., 1990.

Likert, Rensis. *New Patterns of Management.* New York: McGraw-Hill, 1961.

Lytle, William O. *Socio-Technical Systems Analysis & Design Guide: For Linear Work.* New Jersey: Block, Petrella, & Weisbord, Inc., 1991.

Lytle, William O. *Socio-Technical Systems Analysis & Design Guide: For Non-Linear Work.* New Jersey: Block, Petrella, Weisbord, Inc., 1991.

Marshall, Ray & Marc Tucker. *Thinking for a Living: Education & the Wealth of Nations.* New York: Basic Books, 1992.

Mohrman, Susan Albers & Thomas G. Cummings. *Self-Designing Organizations: Learning How to Create High Performance.* New York: Addison-Wesley, 1989.

Nora, John J., C. Raymond Rogers & Robert J. Stamy. *Transforming the Workplace.* New Jersey: Princeton Research Press, 1986.

Orsburn, Jack D., Linda Moran, Ed Musselwhite, & John H. Zenger. *Self-Directed Work Teams: The New American Challenge.* Illinois: Business One Irwin, 1990.

Pasmore, William A. *Designing Effective Organizations: The Sociotechnical Systems Perspective.* New York: John Wiley & Sons, Inc., 1988.

Peters, Tom. *Thriving on Chaos: Handbook for a Management Revolution.* New York: Alfred A. Knopf, 1987.

Team Barriers, Succeeding As a Self-Directed Work Team, SDWTs & Your Organization, Skill-Building for S-D Team Members, and other books/workbooks are available through MW Corporation by calling 914-528-0888. Ask about **QUANTITY DISCOUNTS.** *All orders are shipped same day.*

Schonberger, Richard J. *World Class Manu- facturing Casebook: Implementing JIT and TQC.* New York: The Free Press, 1987.

Waterman, Robert H. *The Renewal Factor.* New York: Bantam Books, 1988.

Wellins, Richard S., William C. Byham, & Jeanne M. Wilson. *Empowered Teams:*

Creating Self-Directed Work Groups that Improve Quality, Productivity, & Participation. San Francisco: Jossey-Bass, 1991.

Weisbord, Marvin R. *Productive Work- places: Organizing & Managing for Dignity, Meaning & Community.* San Francisco: Jossey-Bass, 1987.

VIDEOS

"Team Building: An Exercise In Leadership" (25 min.)

"Empowerment" (22 min.)

"Managing Organizational Change" (25 min.)

"Coaching & Counseling" (25 min.)

"Conflict Management" (25 min.)

"Effective Meeting Skills" (25 min.)

"The Power of Change:" Part I—"The Management Revolution" (16 min.) Part II: "Reinventing the Organization" (30 min.)

"Redesigning a Workplace for Self-Regulation: The Rohm & Haas Story" (34 min.)

"Accelerated Work Redesign" (30 min.)

"The Changing Workplace: Managers, Workers, & Supervisors Speak Out" (32 min.)

"Self-Directed Work Teams" (29 min.)

"Topeka Pride: 20 Years of Self-Direction" (32 min.)

"Cutting Edge Teamwork: A Hi-Tech Company Redesigns" (30 min.)

"Supervisors" (28 min.)

"Supervisor In Transition" (27 min.)

"A Team Leader's Day" (32 min.)

"Everybody Leads: Rotating Team Leadership" (26 min.)

"Improving Work Systems: Redesigning A Service Organization" (27 min.)

"Leading A Service Team: A Day With A High-Performance Work Team Facilitator" (32 min.)

Workplace Teams: Part I—"Building Successful Teams" (26 min.)
　　　　　　　　　　　　Part II—"Helping Your Team Succeed" (26 min.)

Empowerment: Part I—"Empowering Others" (26 min.)
　　　　　　　　　Part II—"Empowering Yourself" (26 min.)

"Keeping Teams Together" (20 min.)

"Motivating Others" (25 min.)

"Coaching for Top Performance" (25 min.)

"Making Diversity Work" (20 min.)

"Time: the Next Dimension of Quality" (20 min.)

"Tools for Continuous Improvement" (Healthcare & Industrial Versions Available)

"Quality Secrets: the Baldrige Award Winners Speak" (25 min.)

All videos are available for preview or purchase by calling MW Corporation at 914-528-0888 for same day shipment. (All previews contain the complete video not excerpts.) Call for a free Training Catalog describing all books, videos, and workshops.

We Would Like To Hear From You:

Call or write to us to let us know how you used this book:

1. What information did you find particularly helpful?

2. What, if anything, would you like to see included in future reprints?

3. What books, articles, other resources have you found helpful?

4. Could people planning change efforts contact/visit you? (If "yes," please provide your name, title, name of organization, address, phone number, and a brief description of your area of knowledge.)

Fax this page to: 914-528-8889

Or write to: MW Corporation
        3150 Lexington Ave.
        Mohegan Lake, New York 10547

Or call (914) 528-0888 and ask for
. Ann or Bob Harper

MW Corporation is a full-service consulting firm offering the following products and services to support your change efforts.

CONSULTING SERVICES/BOOKS/VIDEOS

PUBLIC WORKSHOPS:
(Throughout the U.S.)

Self-Directed Work Teams Workshop
Advanced Self-Directed Work Teams Workshop
The "1990s Manager" Workshop
Supv./Team Leader/Tech. Leader Workshop
Facilitator Workshop
Active Listening Workshop

ON-SITE TRAINING
(Custom-designed)

On all of the above topics plus:
Team Development

Call the team here at MW Corporation to discuss your training plans. We'd be pleased to send you a FREE Training Catalog.

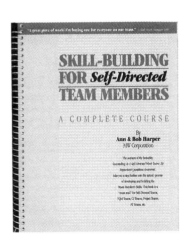

"Redesigning A Workplace for Self-Regulation"   ITEM #V-10

Case Study / Site Visit A UNIONIZED chemical manufacturing plant that has redesigned its entire operation.

In the last 10 years, the Rohm & Haas Chemical Plant in Louisville, Kentucky and its two unions have cooperated and redesigned 18 work units for self-management. This video documents their journey and the dramatic improvements in quality, customer satisfaction and productivity that have come from employee involvement and self-management. See how they did it step-by-step.

1-Week Preview* $45.00   Available in Spanish.
Purchase Price $595.00
Time: 34 min.

"The Changing Workplace"   ITEM #V-3

Ten Managers, Workers, and Supervisors tell how their lives have changed as their companies transition from traditional to participative workplaces. Each group presents their own issues (breakthroughs and challenges) in focusing on teamwork, quality, and learning. This video stimulates important dialog on the benefits of high-performance workplaces and the barriers to overcome. An excellent way for viewers to see the similarities and differences managers, supervisors, and workers generally have when facing the challenge of change.

1-Week Preview* $45.00
Purchase Price $595.00
Time: 32 min.

"Self-Directed Work Teams... Redesigning the Workplace for the 21st Century"   ITEM #V-2000

A "nuts-and-bolts" description of what self-directed teams are and why they make for competitive advantage. Also, how they're different from traditional work in terms of attitudes, skills, etc. This video shows how leadership is handled by teams using a system called, "the star model." You'll see how SDWTs plan the work, schedule it, and improve it. This video helps people at all levels of the organization understand the connection between quality and self-directed teams and see how self-directed teams improve quality, productivity, motivation, etc. An excellent video "overview" of the entire concept of redesigning to SDWTs.

1-Week Preview* $45.00
Purchase Price $550.00
Time: 29 min.

"Topeka Pride"   ITEM #V-9

Case Study / Site Visit See the results of 20 YEARS OF SELF-DIRECTED TEAMS

Learn from one of the most successful applications of self-directed teams. Opened as a "greenfield" production facility in 1971, the Topeka Pet Food factory is America's longest running team-centered work environment. SDWTs on the production floor and in the office manage the day-to-day operations. All Team Members rotate jobs and learn all the skills needed to run this facility as Team Leaders redefine traditional roles.

This video documentary helps people anticipate the growing pains and continual renewal needed to sustain team-based workplaces. A "must see" case study/site visit for any organization thinking about teams, planning for teams, or those who already have teams and want to see what's needed to maintain successful teams that continuously learn and improve.

1-Week Preview* $45.00   Available in Spanish.
Purchase Price $595.00
Time: 32 min.

"Cutting Edge Teamwork"   ITEM #V-11

Case Study / Site Visit A Hi-Tech Company Redesigns for Continuous Learning and Outstanding Quality

StorageTek, a Fortune 500 company, designs and manufactures information storage systems for large mainframe computers. Prior to 1988, StorageTek was having difficulty with the quality of one of their components. Assemblies were failing in the field costing the company millions of dollars. In 1988, they decided to involve their employees in rethinking their work systems. This video shows how their operators, managers, and engineers restructured not only into self-managing teams but extended the concept to cross-functional support teams and shared plant governance. Today, the company produces a product so high in quality that field failures have shrunk to almost zero and their self-designed work system is so successful that many other StorageTek divisions are now emulating it.

1-Week Preview* $45.00
Purchase Price $595.00
Time: 30 min.

*All previews show you the complete video and, if you purchase, preview fee is deducted.